SEX

Dados Internacionais de Catalogação na Publicação (CIP)
(Câmara Brasileira do Livro, SP, Brasil)

Gikovate, Flávio
    Sex / Flávio Gikovate ; [translation Alison Entrekin]. –
São Paulo : MG Editores, 2011.

    Título original: Sexo
    ISBN 978-85-7255-080-2

    1. Conduta de vida 2. Homens – Comportamento sexual
3. Mulheres – Comportamento sexual 4. Sexo (Psicologia) I. Título.

11-03986   CDD-155.3

Índice para catálogo sistemático:

1. Comportamento sexual : Aspectos psicológicos   155.3

No part of this work may be reproduced or transmitted
in any form or by any means, electronic or mechanical,
including photocopying and recording, or by any
information storage or retrieval system without the prior
written permission of Summus Editorial unless such
copying is expressly permitted by federal copyright law.

SEX

Flávio Gikovate

Translated by Alison Entrekin

SEX
Copyright © 2011 by Flávio Gikovate
All rights reserved by Summus Editorial

Translation: **Alison Entrekin**
Cover design: **Alberto Mateus**
Art and design: **Crayon Editorial**

MG Editores
Editorial departament:
Rua Itapicuru, 613 – 7º andar
05006-000 – São Paulo – SP
Brazil
Tel.: (55) (11) 3872-3322
Fax: (55) (11) 3872-7476
http://www.mgeditores.com.br
e-mail: mg@mgeditores.com.br

Printed in Brazil

Introduction

I have been keenly observing developments in sexuality since 1966, the year I graduated from medical school. It is hard to imagine another period of time as short as the last few decades in which so many changes have taken place in the behaviour of entire populations. I saw the introduction of the contraceptive pill and the freedom movements that, in 1968, affected people all over the world and influenced the way of life of a whole generation of young people. Many of them, who were previously more conservative, began to use drugs such as marijuana and cocaine. More recently, there has been an enormous increase in alcohol consumption by young men and – especially – women. I am not ignoring facts with more positive consequences that have also taken place. One such example is the increasing number of young women who invest in their intellectual development in order to become independent professionals. I see casual erotic encounters – "hooking up" – between teenagers of the same social class and age group as a positive thing. I also appreciate certain changes in the sexual initiation of young men:

many now prefer to remain chaste until their first relationship, a situation in which young women also tend to lose their virginity without feeling guilty or ashamed.

I do, however, think it is necessary to separate the things that have proven to be constructive from those that have had negative consequences. I watched the first stirrings of so-called sexual freedom, especially women's. Women gained the freedom to display their bodies, stimulating the fascination of many men and the wrath of some. We believed that greater sexual freedom would bring society more peace and love – and fewer wars. It is not what happened.

More recently, I saw the revolution in sexual – and even romantic – customs introduced by the rising importance of the virtual world: the growth of the porn industry, young men's fascination with all manner of visual stimuli, the tendency of many toward indolence and a lack of interest in studies and "real" girls. I see the extent to which couples' sex lives have been influenced by what they see in porno films, and don't view it favourably. On the other hand, masturbation has clearly gained a "dignity" that it was previously denied, which may lead to some interesting reflection.

The saddest thing for those who, like me, put faith in the prevalent ideals of the late 1960s and 1970s (so well documented by respected authors such as H. Marcuse and W. Reich, among others), is seeing that all these developments have only led to greater dissatisfaction for large portions of society. We are more and more depressed, unhappy, competitive, materialistic and consumerist. I'm not sure we can attribute the sadness that plagues us solely to what has taken place in the realm of sexuality. But it seems that the premise that sexual emancipation would lay the foundations for us to be happier and more solidary, better friends and more competent in matters of love, hasn't proven to be correct in practice.

Ideals that do not work in practice should be abandoned, but it isn't what generally happens. In fact, it is incredible that all these changes haven't been accompanied by real shifts in the way most of us – including psychology professionals – think. Reality has evolved but theory hasn't!

To this day, most people can't, for example, separate sex from love and see that they are different impulses. We are taught that they are part of the same instinct and the belief remains when the facts point to the contrary, even in the minds of the highly educated. Few are the "porous" spirits capable of abandoning old notions, living with doubt and generating new ideas that better explain the facts. While it is already difficult for people to recognise sex and love as separate things, it seems it is even harder to see how sex is related to aggression. This difficulty remains even in the face of the most flagrant evidence, both biological (in the primitive world, more violent males were certainly more competent at copulating with females) and cultural (in so many languages, lewd terms designate maximum verbal violence).

I believe that knowledge should help improve quality of life, individual happiness and the consideration and pleasure we derive from interpersonal relations in general, especially more intimate ones. Beautiful theories that fall short of these objectives should be discarded and replaced with others that can help us develop knowledge that contributes to our well-being.

That is the reason for this book, which brings me back to the subject of my early studies. I consider this rewinding to be essential, since the consequences of our prior convictions have been so negative. Our so-called sexual freedom has ended up intensifying everything it was supposed to fight. We appear to be headed for an abyss. We need to muster up the humility and wisdom to see that it's better to start over, hence such a broad-sounding title – sex. This is my intention.

I know how hard it is when we find ourselves face-to-face with a point of view that is vastly different from the one we are used to. I know how difficult it is to change our paradigms and that we tend to prefer reading things that correspond with our points of view. Nevertheless, I hope that you, dear reader, will indulge and accompany me in these reflections, which, in my view, may provide a new way of looking at sex. Although there are many publications out there, I think there is still much to be done before we can consider sex a well-resolved subject. My aim is to contribute to the discussion with a new perspective. It is a thorny, difficult subject, but I will try to set out my ideas as clearly and succinctly as possible.

1
one

My objective here is to start anew. I believe that ruminations on the subject of sex to date have taken some erroneous turns down dead-end roads. Well-resolved matters tend to be forgotten and aren't discussed as often. We essentially fret over things that aren't going so well. When we're sick, we mostly think about how bad we feel and how to get better. When our health is restored we welcome it back with great pleasure (a negative pleasure, because it corresponds to the end of pain) and it goes back to being less relevant. Sickness is an important topic in our subjectivity, while health isn't.

Sex has unique characteristics due to the fact that it is a positive pleasure; that is, it doesn't require a prior discomfort in order to manifest. We can be doing nothing and suddenly feel the pleasant sensation of arousal. **But sex is also cause for great worry. We doubt our sexual competence or ability to satisfy our partners and worry about whether or not we conform to society's standards of beauty, frequency of sexual relations, the size of our sexual organs, etc.**

And the list doesn't stop here. We want to know if we are making the most of what is nowadays said to be life's greatest pleasure. We want to know if others are doing better in the areas of seduction and sexual conquest, if it is important to have a range of experiences with a variety of partners, if we should masturbate as often as we do, if the pleasure we feel when touching certain parts of our bodies is "normal" or an indication of a fetish, if we should seek to live out our group sex fantasies in real life, and so on.

I know few people who are satisfied with their sex life, who don't feel they are missing out on something by living as they do. The vast majority dream of things that are way out of reach: not all of the circumstances that lead to desire provide the conditions for it to be acted upon. In fact, few people are satisfied with what they have in all of the areas considered important by contemporary culture. Most complain about their physical appearance, their social and financial position, that they have too much (or too little) work, that they are aging and have to live with the external signs of it, as well as growing dietary, alcohol, and other restrictions.

This is an era in which more and more adults have childish character traits stemming from their difficulty dealing with frustration, setbacks and limitations. I'd say the hardest thing of all is coping with limitations and the fact that we weren't born with everything. More than ever I am reminded of something Bertrand Russell once said (sadly, I have lost the original reference) to the effect that the only thing people don't complain about not having enough of is common sense – which he considered the scarcest of attributes.

Sex has also taken similar paths and, as in other areas of life, what we do and the satisfaction we obtain from it are now quantitatively assessed. Most people are under the impression that others are enjoying more sexual pleasure than themselves and are satisfied with their sex lives. This is because few people like to feel outdone and many, as a result, exaggerate their own conquests. They know they're lying, but others tend to believe them. This used to be common among teenagers, but it appears to have spread to all age groups. In this quest for eternal youth, in which ageing appears to be against the rules, we are regressing more and more and are becoming adults with childish characteristics!

It is clear to me that we urgently need to go back to square one in our thinking about sexuality and hone our notions of life and the human condition. Our current way of thinking has produced very negative consequences and the number of depressed, frustrated, unhappy people – even among more privileged sections of society – is growing daily. This is because we live in a world of comparisons in which everyone looks at those who have more and are saddened by what they don't have – instead of being thankful for what they do have. No one's glass is "half full", rather, they are all "half empty".

I am not overlooking the correlation between what goes on in the area of sexuality and what people experience in their social context as a whole. I know how vanity – an important aspect of our sexual instinct – weighs on the yearning (common to us all) to stand out from the crowd. Over the last few decades I have observed an increase in exhibitionism – especially among women – and heightened disputes among men, women and everyone in the dash to obtain more and more money, fame and power. I don't put these things down to coincidence or chance.

I shall try, little by little, to rewrite one of the main subjects of my study and reflection since 1967.

two

Those who wish to think seriously about sexuality need to, before anything else, free themselves of any preconceived ideas. This is very hard, seeing as how, throughout history, sex has always been one of the most regulated subjects. Certain things (i.e. incest) are forbidden in all societies. Requirements such as the sexual fidelity of women were essential in order to guarantee paternity. In other words, and as Freud thought, some kind of limitation (repression) on the full exploration of sexual urges has been indispensable in establishing social organization.

We live in an era in which the limits imposed on sexuality are minimal compared to six decades ago. The taboo that women couldn't lose their virginity before they were married evaporated just a few years after the appearance of the contraceptive pill. Women's economic independence made it possible for them to leave tyrannical or unsuitable husbands. Divorce is now legal in most countries, and discrimination against single people is practically non-existent now – and they have the right to live much freer sex lives. Crimes of passion have become much fewer and farther between, though it doesn't mean people are having fewer extramarital affairs (on the contrary).

At first sight, it would appear that there are fewer prejudices. It may seem that we are living in an era of sexual freedom. However, if we consider a few more things, we will see that it isn't necessarily so: how many families manage not to fret about the virility of a more sensitive son who doesn't like competitive sports such as football? How many parents would let their son study ballet, even if he obviously has the talent for it? How many men feel comfortable if they don't have an erection when getting physically intimate with a new partner whom they like a lot? And how many women dare tell a new partner that they can't achieve orgasm during vaginal penetration and prefer to have their clitoris manually or orally stimulated? How many men feel comfortable asking their partners to stimulate their anal region? And how many women wouldn't interpret it as a sign of homosexual tendencies in their partner?

I could go on, but the list is long enough to illustrate that we still have a long way to go to free ourselves of the prejudices surrounding sex. How many people, men and women, have the courage to "confess" that they prefer masturbation to casual sex – and sometimes even to sex with stable romantic partners? Our society still sees sexual exchanges with others as more pleasurable and relevant than masturbation, but the internet – and erotic material circulating on it – places this point of view in check. **New facts should make people revisit their ideas. But how many are willing to do so?**

We are conservative creatures with a tendency to hold on to old points of view and reject the new. This is how we act towards new electronic devices. We do the same with our beliefs, with the ideas that we inherit ready-made from our parents (who often inherited them from their own parents). In a subject as regulated as sex, few are those who think freely, who produce their own ideas. Some beliefs come from way back, the fruit of religious traditions and society's most deep-rooted prejudices. Others are more recent and have come, for example, from psychoanalytical theories established during the 20th century.

Freud and the first psychoanalysts dared much and confronted the Victorian dogmas that generated a lot of suffering for many people. They liberated many of those who felt guilty for the simple fact of having what were considered inappropriate sexual desires. But these psychoanalysts created new dogmas – or consolidated old ones – that have been blindly obeyed by their followers. Sex and love are still understood as part of the same instinctive impulse (after all, what is the definition of instinct?). There is talk of boys' sexual desire for their mothers, even though children's only manifestations toward their mothers have to do with tenderness and dependence. There is talk of inherent bisexuality to explain the existence of homosexuality, but if that were the case, in an era as free as ours, shouldn't practicing bisexual adults be the majority? Why do straight men still have so many prejudices and fear any kind of physical intimacy with members of the same sex? Gay men have the same prejudices and fear being sexually approached by members of the opposite sex. Why?

Although people have never had so much sex, thought so much about it, produced so much and such varied erotic material, it appears we are still far from a consistent understanding of it. We need to free ourselves of the traditional beliefs that limit our thinking in oft-times imperceptible ways. More than anything, we need to free ourselves of the supposedly definitive scientific knowledge collected in the first half of the 20th century. It is imperative that we understand that all knowledge is historically determined and that the time is now ripe for rethinking the subject. The changes that have taken place, so quickly in so many areas (including sexual intimacy), have fostered the development of skills that may allow us to look at many non-essential issues from a new perspective.

An educator once told me that when our minds are not overloaded with knowledge and information, we are in a very creative state. She called it "creative ignorance". I think I used to be freer in my thinking than I am today, because, in a way, I'm slave to the ideas that I have produced myself thanks to my characteristic ignorance early on in my career as a psychotherapist. I have learned from my patients, from the work that has given me such great pleasure over more than forty years. I will try to free myself as much as possible of the notions that I have already developed on the subject. I ask that you, attentive reader, do the same and try to accompany me on this adventure through the unknown world of sex.

three

I am more and more convinced that there is an urgent need, both theoretical and practical, to distinguish love from sex. Love is what we feel for someone special whose presence brings us pleasant feelings of peace and cosiness – so welcome because it attenuates the feeling of forsakenness that accompanies us from the first moment of extra-uterine life. The harmony of the womb is broken at birth, giving origin to a feeling of incompleteness that stays with us forever. When a newborn baby is cradled by its mother, it feels something similar to what it felt in the "paradise" from which it was expelled. Thus, its first love object is its mother. **Love is, therefore, a negative pleasure – an attenuation of the painful feeling of incompleteness and forsakenness. It is equivalent to a feeling of peace and harmony and depends on the presence of another person. It is an interpersonal phenomenon par excellence. From this perspective, it is impossible to love oneself.**

Later in life, mothers tend to be replaced by other figures. The basic characteristics of the phenomenon are all there, however, similar to the ones that manifest in very early life. Loving oneself, self-respect and self-esteem are completely distinct terms. The first doesn't actually exist; the second has to do with vanity – which we also like to refer to as pride; and the third has to do with the way we see ourselves and is thus a phenomenon intermediated by reason, which depends on a pre-existing code of values.

Sex takes a completely different route to the one described above. Its first manifestations appear a little later, around the end of the first year of life. They are concomitant with a child's realization that its mother is a separate person ("psychological birth"). In this phase, children try to explore everything around them, as well as themselves, as much as possible. They put anything they can in their mouths to see what they taste like and touch objects and themselves. They realize that touching certain parts of the body can spark pleasant sensations and vibrations – and a kind of restlessness, which they experience as pleasurable. This pleasurable restlessness will later be called sexual arousal, and the parts of the body that give rise to it are the erogenous zones.

Children's discovery of sex is part of the process of getting to know themselves and the world around them. It is a phenomenon related to the first steps in the building of one's individuality. It takes place without the interference of other beings. Sexual arousal is the product of individual activity and, for this reason, is referred to as autoerotic. Sex is thus arousal, not peace; it is a positive pleasure because it doesn't de-

pend on the existence of prior discomfort that is attenuated by its manifestation (as is the case when a child is crying and is cheered up when its mother comes over), **and it is an essentially personal phenomenon.**

Mindful of these three elements (interpersonal or personal; positive or negative pleasure; and the kinds of feelings they cause), it is easy to see that not only are sex and love not the same thing, but they don't even belong to a single instinctive phenomenon. They are, more than anything, opposing! It is not surprising, therefore, that reconciling these two elements of our subjectivity is, even as adults, quite difficult.

I often wonder why so many extraordinary scholars of human psychology have committed such a terrible mistake. From the little I know, religious thinkers (of all creeds and eras) have always looked at love favourably, though the same cannot be said of sex. The idea of limiting its practice to reproductive needs appears to have been a strong feature of their thinking, which has indirectly implied attempts to keep its influence to a necessary minimum. I imagine that they believed sexual freedom had the power to disrupt family life (seen as essential) and to generate conduct that was inconvenient for the smooth running of life in society. At some stage in the following pages, it will become clear that I suspect they weren't entirely wrong.

Such great efforts to repress sexual impulses may well be responsible for two simultaneous phenomena:

an increase in the relative importance of sex, making it the theme of fantasies and daydreams for the vast majority of people; and the production of psychological disturbances and somatic symptoms in people who are less competent at managing and controlling their fantasies. It was precisely in one such era of sexual repression, most specifically in the late 19th and early 20th centuries, that Freud developed his ideas. They couldn't fail to be liberating in nature, trying to lighten the repression weighing on the subject of sex.

I understand up to this point. But attributing an erotic nature (related to the presence of an obvious sexual desire) to the strong emotional ties that children, especially boys, have with their mothers strikes me as mistaken; if it exists, it is an exception rather than a rule. Boys feel intense love for their mothers and want to be close to them so they can feel sheltered and cosy. Even when they suck at their mothers' breasts, they do not have erotic feelings; rather, they are loving in nature. Freud's oral phase strikes me as essentially emotional, at least during early childhood. This is in keeping with what can be observed.

The marriage between sex and love, transforming the latter into a sublimated (sugary-sweet and more grandiose) version of the former, probably arose out of theoretical musings rather than observable facts. I perfectly understand the tendency to accommodate ideas so that they form a body of coherent concepts. What I can't accept is that it be done to the detriment

Flávio Gikovate

of the facts. The facts must speak louder. When a girl feels sexual arousal when she jumps onto her father's thigh with her legs open, it doesn't mean she desires him. All it means is that her erogenous zone was stimulated as a result of her action. If she had jumped onto the arm of a sofa, she'd feel exactly the same thing, but it would be unreasonable to think she feels sexual desire for the sofa.

At any rate, the most relevant thing that happened in the early years of psychoanalysis was, in my opinion, Freud's ability (and that of many of his followers) to assign the correct importance to the phenomenon of sex. It is one of the most intricate aspects of our subjectivity. The changes that have taken place since the 1960s (thanks to, among other things, the appearance of the contraceptive pill) have only reinforced its importance in the personal and social lives of all. We have also learned, in my view, that we know very little about the matter – and still have a long way to go before we can dream of knowing even the basics of how sexuality is processed in our species.

four

I would now like to discuss another basic concept that I consider fundamental: the difference between arousal and desire. **The feeling usually referred to as "desire" is key to contemporary understandings of sexuality – and subjectivity in general. Here, once again, we find ourselves facing a dangerous problem: the imprecise use of generic terms.** None of us are mind readers, and it is essential that we seek to be as clear as possible in our communication so that we all have a chance at understanding one another. Dialects and jargon are inappropriate for the study of important subjects regarding human peculiarities, whether from the point of view of psychology, philosophy, sociology, anthropology, etc. Elitism hinders comprehension and also isolates lay members of society who would like to understand themselves and their peers better, and who should be able to play the important role of critical observers.

I propose that we define desire as a longing to approach or have someone or something that is external

Flávio Gikovate

to us.[1] **In the case of sexual desire, the objective is to get physically close to another person in order to exchange caresses that can lead to ejaculation or the female orgasm. Desire needs to be differentiated from need: when a baby cries and wants to be physically close to its mother, it is feeling poorly for some reason and needs its mother to comfort it and make its feeling of forsakenness go away.**

Obviously, the difference between desire and need isn't hard and fast. A child may want to be picked up even when he or she isn't feeling bad. They might like the cosiness of it. However, in its origin, it is a negative pleasure, something that exists to attenuate some kind of ill feeling. The same thing happens with our need to eat: it can, through the interference of our minds, turn into a desire (or craving) for a specific kind of food prepared in a very particular way. Thirst can be quenched with water (a need), but also with juices and soft drinks with special flavours (a desire that has grown out of a need). Desires of this kind are cultural constructs that sophisticate organic needs essential to our survival.

Desire is related to the optional, while needs correspond to the indispensable. We construct desires out of needs, but only the latter must be satisfied. Sexual desire is thus the only kind of desire that is genuinely

---

[1] There is a subtle difference between "desiring" something and "wanting" something. The latter is more generic and encompasses a range of psychological manifestations that can lead to some kind of approximation which, as a rule, have been the object of some kind of rational – or even moral – consideration. Desire implies more spontaneous, autonomous acts.

Flávio Gikovate

biological, inherent and spontaneous in all of us. Many material desires are a product of their era and culture. They spring from our intelligence and creativity and can easily latch onto those of an erotic nature. I will return to this point shortly.

During childhood there are no obvious manifestations of the presence of erotic desires. It is common, however, to see children touching their erogenous zones in order to feel the pleasant restlessness that we call sexual arousal. Arousal isn't the same thing as desire, because desire implies an object. The only way to treat arousal and desire as the same thing would be for us to be objects. We would be subject and object of our sexual arousal, which would be synonymous with self-desire. I am not partial to this line of thinking, which seems to require unnecessary intellectual gymnastics. I have already mentioned the fact that, having separated love and sex, there is also no point thinking that children have sexual desires for their parents. I don't think desire exists where there is need – except the culturally constructed kind mentioned above.

I think it is essential that we distinguish between two types of erotic manifestation, not only in childhood, but also adult life. **Sexual arousal is an inner phenomenon that takes place inside us – sparked or not by thoughts involving other people. Sexual desire incites movement toward the object of desire. Male sexual desire clearly**

Flávio Gikovate

emerges in puberty: boys are visually stimulated by girls' bodies, faces and expressions. This happens when they see real girls, when they look at suggestive pictures or even when they imagine or remember the female body in erotic positions or situations. I am speaking, obviously, about what happens in a heterosexual context. In a gay context, the object of desire is same-sex. We will come back to this important aspect of human sexuality.

Arousal takes place in our subjectivity and doesn't require external objects. It occurs in and of itself, an essentially personal phenomenon without a direct relationship to desire. It doesn't require action. **Even in adult life, the presence of sexual desire in women cannot be clearly observed, at least as a rule. They are the object of men's desire, and men – in turn – are always tuned in to their gestures, the details of their bodies, to what they can furtively observe of their private parts. Women are well aware of it and are turned on by the fact that they feel desired. Being the object of someone's desire feels good and, naturally, they will actively seek it over the years.** However, most women don't appear to have an overt obsession with specific parts of men's bodies. Even when they appreciate certain details, I don't believe they experience the same signs of arousal that men do. **It should be said here that desire also leads to arousal, but clearly sparked by an external object with which maximum proximity is intended, and actively pursued (sometimes even inconveniently).**

Flávio Gikovate

Until just a few years ago most men were highly frustrated that they weren't desired the way they desired women. This generated anger and indignation, not to mention envy of women. I believe this is the root of sexism, a male resource that has always tried to minimize men's condition of sexual inferiority via their greater physical strength and supposed intellectual superiority. This is in the process of being overcome, and I don't think it is worth going into in any depth. Men are less frustrated today because many women, even though they don't feel the same kind of desire, are bolder in making the first move.

I think it is too soon to assume that it has to do with a desire on the part of women that has been repressed throughout the centuries. It wouldn't have been in men's interest to impede something that they so longed for. What they did was precisely the contrary: they forbade women to show their bodies! In some instances, they were allowed to show their eyes – and only because they had to be able to see to walk. What has happened is that men are more laid back and less slave to their desire. Women, on the other hand, have taken more efficient initiatives to allow men to approach them, which they now long for more than men do. I am not referring so much to sexual approaches, which men have always been more interested in, but to sentimental ones (even if disguised as sexual).

I have only observed sexual arousal in children. Even when there is an exchange of caresses between

Flávio Gikovate

two boys, two girls or a boy and a girl, everything suggests that they are only imitating what they have observed in the adult world. There may be some casual curiosity about the functioning of sexuality – and the sexual organs of other children, but I don't believe it is indicative of any kind of desire or even subtracts from the autoerotic nature of these sexual experiments, in which interaction is very superficial.

Throughout adult life, two relevant ingredients hinder the observation of sexual phenomena. The first is the connection that this instinctive impulse establishes with the essentially interpersonal phenomena of aggressiveness and love. The second is the previously-mentioned emergence of male visual desire, which gives a strong appearance of interactivity to a process that, during childhood, doesn't manifest as such. Visual desire is not usually present in women, but strong manifestations of arousal can be observed in them when they realize they are desired. In spite of all the critical discourse of the 1970s and 80s, everything appears to suggest that women really like being seen as sexual objects!

Summarizing what has been discussed to this point, we can say that we are motivated by needs as well as desires – intermediated by our minds and produced by culture – which latch on to them. Love belongs to the realm of need. The main expression of sex, at least during childhood, is arousal, which is a personal phenomenon and manifests individually. In an early phase, it is an essentially tactile pleasure, derived from the stimulation – direct or intermediated by a partner – of the erogenous zones. With puberty, male sexual desire – and the urge to get close to and rub up against the female body that provoked it – really kicks in; the objective is to relieve the intense arousal that arose as a result of what the boy saw as well as what he felt through direct contact with the woman's erogenous zones.

The lack of visual desire on the part of women puts them in a privileged position, in which they become aroused when they realize that they are the object of male desire. They are desired by men and don't desire them back in the same way. As a result, they are in a better position to carefully chose which ones they will be open to and which they will reject. Men are left in the humiliating position of having to subject themselves to this kind of selection process.

On the other hand, if women are aroused when they realize they are desired, it stands to reason that they may feel very frustrated if it doesn't happen. This pleasure isn't distributed democratically, and less attractive women hurt when their wish to be desired goes unrealized! Wanting to provoke desire brings us back to the question of vanity, an erotic ingredient that we will look at next.

five

Human sexuality cannot be seriously studied without taking into account a curious ingredient that first appears at around the ages of 5 or 6: we feel enormous pleasure when we attract the attention of the people around us and receive their admiration. When successful, children feel something equivalent to what they feel when they touch their erogenous zones, perhaps a little more diffuse: a generalized excitement perceived as highly pleasant. Like with any pleasurable sensation, there is a tendency, intermediated by reason, to try to reproduce similar situations so the pleasure is repeated. If a child's new watch earns him looks of surprise and admiration, it is reasonable to expect that he will desire other adornments capable of producing the same excitement derived from the reaction of admiration of those around them – regardless of who they are.

The erotic pleasure of showing off requires one to stand out from the crowd, to be different to the majority. During childhood, the wish to be a part of large groups (family, schoolmates, neighbours, etc.) has a strong effect on the desire to stand out from the crowd. The desire is always present, but only manifests occa-

sionally. **In other words, the need to feel integrated – and cosy – predominates over the desire to stand out.** As a result, manifestations of vanity are discreet, and exhibitionism often manifests in the realm of fantasy: boys and (especially) girls dress up in adult clothes and pose extravagantly in the bedroom mirror. They are able to imagine the impact they would cause, but don't dare do so in front of real observers. **What we do in the mirror can be considered equivalent to masturbation as far as vanity is concerned.**

Then comes puberty and, with it, the erotic longings of adulthood. Teenage boys want to get physically close to the girls that stimulate strong visual desire in them. Girls realize that boys desire them, but that they are not affected in the same way by the presence of boys. They feel extremely aroused when they realize how coveted they are; but they don't feel the same. They end up allowing the more insistent boys, who are usually also the most aggressive and rude, to approach them. There is, thus, a certain logic to the traditional – and highly sexist – male theory that girls, when duly chased, might just give in to temptation!

Even without feeling desire, the fact is that the intense arousal that comes from being coveted makes girls fragile, and if they don't have much self-control, they may, in fact, lose control. When they understand the process better, however, they become more and more familiar with the intensity of their arousal and their fear of losing control fades. They slowly free themselves of it.

Flávio Gikovate

The loss of fear ushers in a wish to provoke the desire of a growing number of men. This stimulates the exhibitionist pleasure of vanity, now accompanied by a large component of well-defined sexual arousal. The diffuse erotic pleasure derived from exhibitionism in childhood takes on much more concrete contours and its objective is exhibiting one's own body, often decorated with special adornments capable of stimulating desire in boys (and men in general) even more.

From this point, reason begins to participate more actively in the mechanisms related to our sexuality. Nothing in us is exclusively biological, just as cultural procedures that don't contain an element of our biology are also rare. We are biopsychosocial beings, and it would be highly reductionist to try to play down the importance of any of our characteristics. Our reason is influenced by biology and culture; based on these things, it makes its own decisions, but in most cases the main influence comes from prevailing cultural beliefs.

Nowadays, overt female exhibitionism is the cultural standard. Since the end of the 1960s, women's right to behave as they please has been one of the ideals related to the freedom movements – stemming from their growing economic independence and the invention of the contraceptive pill. **The male right – exacerbated by traditional religions – to control what and how much women can show of themselves has crumbled, at least in the West.**

Sex
Flávio Gikovate

Women can freely exercise their vanity, which is dominated by the wish to become aroused by provoking male desire. They can use all manner of resources for this purpose: taking care of their bodies, weight, skin and hair. They are stimulated by publicity that always promises better results in the process of seduction. They begin to desire objects capable of increasing their powers: provocative shoes, beach wear that shows as much as possible of their bodies (which they work out with great dedication), low-cut evening-wear that exhibits their recently augmented breasts, and so on. **They don't desire men, but are highly aroused by the desire they provoke in them, such that they long for the objects and resources that can increase the pleasure derived from a good result in men's eyes. This is how the enormous consumer appetite – almost unheard of just a few decades ago, though partially due to a lack of objects to be consumed – arose.**

The urge to buy adornments capable of further stimulating male desire is an important factor in women's arousal. They feel attracted to such objects; they want to own them, have them near their bodies. The urge to purchase consumer items has obviously spilled over beyond this aspect of our psychology, and goods that define status and social condition are also sought after: handbags, watches and other objects that men are not terribly interested in – but which inspire envy in other women. We have also seen a significant increase in consumerism on the part of men, who engage in a dispute that mostly involves so-called "status symbols", which define their position on the social ladder. This is a very complex subject. I am no expert in it and this isn't the moment to discuss it exhaustively.

Men are in quite a different situation to women. Women are exploring new frontiers, while men are somewhat perplexed and withdrawn. They are strongly provoked by women, who benefit from the elaborate paraphernalia they have at their disposal to make themselves even more attractive. During the 1980s, when the process became more evident and intense, men sought professional success so as to neutralize women's growing sensual power. In so doing, they used a traditional formula: attractive women tended to succumb to the overtures of powerful men, who went to great efforts to become powerful while they were still young. This phase, which was trying and terrible for men, was perhaps responsible for a period of economic growth, as well as the amount of consumer items at the disposal of a growing number of people. Women reacted and began to participate more actively in the job market, to such an extent that today they are the majority in universities, at least in the West.

Younger men – those who entered adolescence in the 1990s – have been affected by a big, unexpected development which is often referred to as "hooking up": boys and girls of the same age and social class began to engage erotically with one another in a simple, casual way. From this point on, young men became

Flávio Gikovate

less willing to play the traditional game in which economic and social power belonged to men and sensual power, to women. They also started to work on their physical appearance and, like young women, spend hours and hours working out at gyms – which can be found on every street corner and are frequented by a growing number of people. They also use moisturizers and get liposuction. They have become somewhat lazy as regards studies, because they are no longer terribly optimistic about their chances of success with women through this avenue. They have always desired them, and that used to be the driving force behind their efforts to be financially successful. They also compete among themselves to see who is most successful – and this dispute may have, in many cases, gone way beyond what was necessary for their erotic conquests. Once again I shall stop here, as I am not an expert on this specific subject.

A recent thing that has caught my attention is that the existence of visual desire in young men may be keeping them away from their female counterparts. This is because the technological advances have given them a wealth of free and easy-to-access erotic material on the internet. The virtual world has grown radically in the last twenty years, and visual stimuli of an erotic nature – of great intensity – are at the disposal of whomever wants them. The virtual world is much more attractive to young men than to women, since they are the ones who are aroused by visual stimuli. We may well be, as a result of this unexpected variable, watching the appearance of phenomena of extreme relevance to the future of interpersonal relationships in decades to come. I will come back to this fundamental subject when I have covered a few more things.

For now, here is another summary of what I have been describing: we are made up of natural needs and desires. Satisfying our needs is essential to our survival. They may be tailored to each era and culture, and may encompass desires we have created ourselves. The natural desire for excellence is sexual in nature – more specifically visual – and only exists in men. Women are aroused when they feel desired, a condition that has grown increasingly privileged due to the freedom to exhibit their bodies that came with their emancipation. The urge to activate this kind of arousal has increased, along with the desire to purchase products and goods capable of making them even more attractive. **Women desire these products and don't desire men. Men, in turn, have started giving up trying to win them over with their professional and financial success. They try to impress women with their physical appearance, which is reasonably effective and attracts their attention because it is a new cultural value; but it doesn't incite desire in them.** Men allow themselves to be impressed by women less and less, delving into the virtual world to intensively realize their desires of a visual nature. The virtual world seems, for the first time, to favour men, resulting in a tendency among younger men to be increasingly apathetic and less willing to chase real women (among other things). Women are exhibiting themselves like never before and men are keeping to themselves like never before!

six

Let us speculate a little about what we'd be like if we were purely biological in an effort to understand some fundamental aspects of different kinds of sexual behaviour, especially their correlation to aggression. In the early 1990s I began pointing out this strong association, which can potentially lead to the wrong romantic choices – after all, lots of people confuse sexual arousal with romantic attraction.

In my reflections on the subject, I have always considered the association between sex and aggression – usually on the part of men – to be very relevant. The strongest kind of verbal aggression is swear words describing violent sexual situations, almost always involving two men. It is interesting to note that these terms are present in all languages. I am increasingly convinced that there is an important innate ingredient, perhaps part of the male hormonal make up. I believe this aggressive trait is related to instinctive actions whose purpose was to perpetuate the species: in primitive times, males had to chase after females who weren't always available and approach them sexually – even without their consent.

Flávio Gikovate

From an evolutionary point of view[2], the most daring and aggressive men would have reproduced more frequently, because they would have approached a larger number of women more vigorously and firmly. In primitive times (scientists say our species has been around for more than 150 thousand years, while we have only led a more organized social life for, say, 10 thousand), life was extremely difficult for women and their children. There were probably many more men than women – which, of course, further increased the chances that those who managed to copulate were really the more aggressive ones. In such a context, it is also not unlikely that the children who inherited these more violent characteristics were, in turn, better adapted to harsh lifestyles, full of adversities; as a result, they would have had greater chances of developing, reaching adulthood and reproducing, increasingly concentrating the aggressiveness in our species, including sexually.

From this point of view, we need to see sex as a separate phenomenon to love. It is also clear that this personal phenomenon has a far greater connection to aggressiveness than to tenderness and affection. As I have stated elsewhere, I consider sex to be a personal phenomenon. It becomes interpersonal when an inter-

---

[2] In order to understand our biology, I believe it is important to consider the thinking of those who, in psychology and sociology, have been influenced by Darwin's theories. What intrigues me is how naively these same people have neglected other ingredients, especially related to life in society and the influence of culture on human beings and their biology. Though I recognise that biology comes to bear on social norms, I also think that they acquire specific peculiarities and take on their own life.

personal ingredient is associated. Aggressiveness is interpersonal in nature: one feels anger or hostility towards someone else. A man chasing after a woman who tries to give him the slip will feel humiliation, in addition to desire, which generates anger. These negative feelings give rise to the first interpersonal manifestations of our eroticism. Our first erotic expressions are, therefore, not at all romantic!

When I think about our species, I always take into consideration the fact that we have complex intellectual properties; additionally, even before the sophistication derived from the acquisition of a language shared by many people (which coincides with the beginning of life in more or less organized, stable society), our psychological equipment was already active. Consider women, who were vulnerable because they were physically weaker. They had few means to avoid being constantly and indiscriminately approached by men – stronger and more aggressive – who desired them. It is impossible to imagine a more tragic beginning for them. I believe that the only reason they didn't harbour bigger grudges was because they didn't imagine other possibilities for existence and because life, especially theirs, wasn't long enough for them to understand what happened to them. **I don't, however, write off the possibility of an important aggressive ingredient in women's subjectivity too. I don't know if it might be attributed to biological causes or if it is the consequence of psychological aspects arising** from their circumstances. However, I do think there was underlying resentment and that, in one way or another, it persisted until not so very long ago.

I also believe that the first favourable change for women took place when certain cavemen decided to take particular women as their own. It may seem strange to refer to that as a step forward for women, but compared to their previous situation, they now had to obey just one man and be sexually available to him only. In turn, it was this man's responsibility to protect the woman and keep her safe from all other men. Perhaps the first rudimentary sentimental ties formed as a result of cohabitation. These fierce men now watched their children grow up – and, perhaps for the first time, were aware and certain that they were their own children. They brought food for everyone, greatly increasing the women and children's chances of survival. I imagine that the first ties of tenderness were being born, the first clear signs of civilization. That is, the first embryos of what later came to be called love were born, and with them the first signs that it would be possible to organize group life in which each woman "belonged" to a man.[3]

It is not impossible that, in spite of the obvious advances, women still developed strong resentment stem-

---

[3] I am not qualified to affirm that the main ingredients impacting social order were of an economic nature, connected to the organization of agricultural production and hunting, or those related to the rudiments of family life in which the first relevant manifestations of love appeared. At any rate, from a psychological point of view, I think that the life that we can truly call "human" began when manifestations of emotional attachment appeared.

ming from their condition of submission. This resentment came to have an even more defined target: the particular man they lived with, whom they had to obey and for whom they had to be sexually available.

7
seven

Our biological characteristics undoubtedly interfere in social organization. The more primitive the society, perhaps the greater the influence of biology. The greater the weight of a particular biological component, the greater its ability to influence the way that even "sophisticated" social groups such as today's are organized. **I believe that the connection between sex and aggression is very deeply rooted and extremely hard to undo.**[4] Currently, families still fret about the virility of less aggressive sons. They encourage them to fight, hit anyone who hits them, or at least defend themselves.

For many fathers – and mothers – it is still very important that their children are good at competitive sports, admire violent superheroes, don't show any interest in traditional women's activities, such as housework or even cooking (as adults, many men develop a taste for it and are even encouraged to take it

---

[4] I never consider a condition to be definitive, because I don't think like Freud, for whom biology was destiny. We don't know what the future holds. No one ever imagined that sex would come to be so definitively separated from reproduction, which happened because of the technological and cultural advances that gave rise to the contraceptive pill. This is just one example of how we are always capable of producing new things and reinventing ourselves.

up), don't appreciate more feminine games, and don't take an interest in artistic activities. **The same wives who complain about their husbands' rude behaviour encourage its equivalent in their sons. This kind of inconsiderate, sexist man is reproduced because of this female contradiction stemming from the fear that more loving, less aggressive, less competitive sons will invariably have an "inappropriate" homosexual destiny.**

Boys with a more violent streak tend to make politer, more sensitive ones the object of all manner of ridicule, usually questioning their "victims'" virility. The kids at school make fun of them and treat them like untouchables. These boys complain to their parents, who, instead of standing up for them and explaining that a lot of people have a pre-historic mind-set, scold them and tell them to give the bullies a taste of their own medicine. The boys can't do it and, deep down, become more and more convinced that their classmates are right, since even their own parents think like them. They develop a growing feeling of inferiority and grow up riddled with doubt about their own sexuality.

They also grow up with a great deal of resentment – both towards the kids who humiliated them and towards their parents who didn't stand up for them, especially their fathers. They grow up with strong hostility towards male figures and full of doubt about their own virility. The result is predictable, but will be discussed at length further along.

Flávio Gikovate

Girls were, until very recently, treated like second-class citizens. Less was demanded of them, precisely because less was expected of them. They were treated with a certain contempt and lack of consideration, but, at the same time, they were more sheltered. Many grew up unhappy with their lot. In other words, the idea that there were two distinct genders defined by the presence or absence of a penis – which they became aware of in the second year of life – gave girls a less exciting, less brilliant fate. **As a result, many developed strong envy and hostility towards boys, which Freud very appropriately named "penis envy".**

Freud considered this manifestation of envy to be universal, which experience doesn't confirm. Everything suggests that there have always been girls who have accepted their condition very well because they identified positively with their mothers, who, in turn, were often happy with and accepting of the lifestyle allocated to women in their particular culture. We have seen drastic cultural changes in the upbringing of girls and boys, which leads me to believe that everything professionals in the humanities thought up until 1970 should be rigorously revisited. The condition of girls today is so different to that of their mothers that we have seen the absolute, radical "victory" of women in what has been dubbed the "war of the sexes".

It should be said that masculinity and femininity should never be considered in isolation, because changes in women's behaviour have a direct repercussion on men, and vice-versa. There is a complex dynamic of changes that even the keenest observers sometimes have a hard time keeping up with. Additionally, it has always been very hard to understand exactly how femininity came to be what it is: how much of it was produced by women themselves and how much was imposed on them by the men who dominated them for millenniums. Let us try to understand – at least a little bit better – the great unknown quantity of psychology: women!

It is easy to explain why men find it so difficult to understand women (and vice-versa). It is hard to assess the subjectivity of beings who are different to ourselves in a more than a certain number of ways. Most women are unable to fully understand what goes on in the minds of men, permanent "victims" of the visual stimuli that they provide. Many women, perhaps the most arbitrary, like to incite desire in men, but don't accept that their partners are attracted to and look at other women. Some are discreet in the name of coherence, that is, because they don't want their partners to show desire for exhibitionists. Others are discreet because they are afraid of the desire they awaken. This fear may be related to the real risk that men will come onto them in an aggressive manner. It may also derive from the fact that they don't feel strong enough to resist a more insistent individual, which excites them because it provides a strong stimulus for their vanity.

I believe that, in the history of civilization, men have always been afraid that women were unable to remain faithful, given the erotic opportunities afforded them by their condition as objects of desire. While in primitive times they were subject to the arbitrary approaches of however many men desired them, after they began to pair up with men, they had protectors and providers – authoritarian and arbitrary, but able to keep other men at bay. **They were the "property" of their protectors. It didn't mean, however, that they stopped being attractive to other men, a condition seen as dangerous for two reasons: firstly, because men have always had their doubts about women's ability to act based on logic (which was thought to be weaker, or inferior in women) and secondly, because, imagining themselves in women's shoes, they believed it would be hard to resist the temptations on offer.**

To this already complex situation, we can also add the important observation that women are not unavailable for sex even after satisfying, orgasmic intercourse. After ejaculation, men experience a period of satiation in which they may feel sleepy and adverse to erotic intimacy. This permanent availability (the absence of a refractory period[5] after orgasm for most women) may have been even more frightening to men, who were more and more inclined to oppress women and hide them from their rivals. This may also have given origin, in many traditional religions, to the practice of adult women covering themselves as much as possible, espe-

---

[5] This term was coined by Masters and Johnson, who pioneered research into the human sexual response from 1957 until the early 1990s. They found that men undergo a refractory period following orgasm, during which they are not able to ejaculate again. Women experience no such period.

cially their hair – which must have been seen as extremely erotic.

All of these actions betray a male belief that, sexually speaking, according to the social order they had built, the power now lay in women's hands. In primitive times, they had no power whatsoever. **However, in any kind of social organization in which a woman is linked to a "protector", she owes him obedience and it is up to him to go out of his way to ensure that other men do not approach her. Wherever there are rules and prohibitions, anxiety about the breaking of these same rules always arises!**

This is especially true among the most powerful members of a social group; they set the rules but aren't too keen to follow them. They are the behaviour police and expect the majority to respect norms, while they grant themselves more rights and greater freedom of action.

The realization that women had acquired enormous power due to their ability to incite male visual desire, a power that could only be neutralized by an active stance on the part of men (stopping them from circulating freely, limiting the use of provocative clothes, etc.), no doubt left them feeling perplexed and unexpectedly fragile – compared to their previous condition of absolute advantage. I believe they went even further: as much as possible, they also stopped women from fully exploring their intellectual potential and participating in any activities seen as socially relevant.

They tried to limit women's sensual power and increase their own social and economic power. They occupied public space and excluded women from all important decision-making processes. They treated them as less qualified and intellectually limited; using all of the devices of the sexism that reigned until just a few decades ago and which has left still-strong marks in the contemporary world. As is to be expected, many women rebelled against the arbitrariness imposed by men. They developed penis envy, which doesn't have anything to do with penises themselves, but with the social privileges attributed to their owners. Many girls were saddened by their own genital anatomy, deducing that their "missing organ" meant they were allocated a secondary role in life.

In addition to the biological predispositions that most certainly make women more competent at looking after babies, a set of domestic obligations was imposed on them that could well have been shared (along with many of the tasks of child rearing). Domestic chores – seen as less relevant – came to be the domain of women. Games and even more serious activities were aimed at preparing girls for their future roles (the same thing happened with boys[6]). **Boy's chores, however, were seen as more important, such that a specific mode of**

---

[6] According to American anthropologist Ruth Benedict, boys were trained from childhood to hunt, for example. She was a staunch advocate for maintaining cultural conditioning, as opposed to societies that don't prepare their children for what they will experience as adults.

behaviour – gender – came to be associated with the male sex. The female gender came to be associated with the female sex, that is, culturally conditioned behaviour based on specific notions of women's nature – but determined by men!

Sex is biological, while gender depends on each culture. Many girls – perhaps the most non-conformist, questioning and impatient – rebelled against the games specific to their gender and decided they preferred activities considered to be the domain of boys. Those who accepted their gender better were able to entertain themselves with the domestic arts and didn't develop any kind of penis envy. In 21st-century societies, where, fortunately, gender differences are fading, this kind of envy may become less and less common. At any rate, non-conformist behaviour on the part of women regarding gender-assigned roles is part of an entirely natural reaction to male arbitrariness stemming from men's traditional insecurity and fear of what might happen if women were freer, in charge of their own destiny and in full possession of the sensual power that men so envy in them. That is, male envy deriving from the fact that they are not desired by women as much as they desire them existed prior to penis envy (penis envy being the consequence of the arbitrariness to which women are subjected because of men's envy of them). **The original envy is male, now on the wane thanks to the homogenization of the genders: there is no longer typically male behaviour in opposition to typically female behaviour.**

Flávio Gikovate

Within this scenario, it makes sense that it has always been impossible to answer the question: "what do women want?" They could only want to be free of male oppression. They have used subtle or obvious means, depending on their degree of emotional maturity and sensitivity, to improve their lot. They have used sensual power, discovered in the first years of adolescence, to humiliate the boys who inspired so much envy in them when they were younger. They have used their charm and sensuality to try to find good romantic partners and, within their relationships, be heard and take part in important decisions regarding family life. Few have been daring and irreverent enough to live outside socially-imposed norms, seeking the kind of individual freedom that only used to be compatible with a solitary life: these women became nuns, artists, revolutionaries and writers; some also voluntarily prostituted themselves in search of freedom – most prostitutes in the past took this path involuntarily, as they were excluded from family life for bad sexual conduct.

Over the next few decades, we will have a better idea of what they really want. For now, they are quite lost and often copy the male model, using it as a reference – which is inadequate and not very creative, since they are adopting the behavioural standards of their traditional oppressors. We do not know how they are going to behave in the face of the sexual, social and economic freedom that they have achieved in the last forty years. I don't think they even know themselves. They

Flávio Gikovate

are aware that there are certain complex and perhaps unexpected problems, among which the fact that men are at odds with the idea of living and working with women they admire and who should be treated as equals. They realize that things are not even that simple sexually: many men run from more exuberant women, always with the traditional fear that they won't be able to keep them satisfied, because they see women as superior in this area – including quantitatively, which is so relevant to men, because they realize that women are interminably available, which they themselves are not.

I am not even considering here the sexual issues concerning potentially good-quality emotional relationships, perhaps one of the most difficult problems to solve in the near future. This is because sex and aggression are so strongly associated with one another in men, as a result of both biological aspects and cultural conditioning. **As such, it is very hard for men to physically desire women who inspire admiration and tenderness in them. They confuse it with a lack of romantic attraction and avoid precisely the ones with whom they could establish the best emotional ties. This is, perhaps, the most serious sub-product of the monumental error we have made in considering love and sex to be parallel phenomena. In practice, they are antagonistic.** Maybe understanding this error fully will help us overcome the obstacle.

I am truly convinced that, for our species, there are no obstacles that cannot be overcome. We are strong enough from a rational and social point of view to find solutions for even the most complex dilemmas imposed by our biology. It is with this mindset that I continue to seek the clarity that can help make us all a little happier.

nine

Let's return to childhood for a bit. The psychoanalytical idea that sexuality manifests before puberty is easily confirmed. All one needs to do is consult their own memory. However, I am increasingly convinced that we need to distinguish between what is sexual and what is emotional. Love-related matters always contain an element of need, of remedying something bad that is affecting the child – and later the adult. If a child is playing and hurts herself, she will immediately run to her mother's cosy arms. There is nothing erotic in this effort to re-establish calm through tender contact. **Tenderness involves physical manifestations very similar to those of an erotic nature. The subjective feeling is completely different, however, and we all know how to distinguish between the two.**

We know, but it seems that the generations that preceded us didn't. The most obvious example of this confusion, very serious in all senses, was the fact that fathers in the past (those who had children before the 1970s) didn't kiss their boys for fear of sending them signals of a homosexual nature. They were denied kisses of tenderness, so necessary in order to feel loved, in the name of ensuring their virility. Those generations didn't know how to distinguish between tenderness and sexual arousal. They deprived their sons of the physical affection they needed to feel good about themselves because of the prevalent beliefs of the time, which early 20th-century psychology took on board.

Children need lots of love and affection, because is helps them to grow up with greater self-confidence. Sex manifests through manipulation of the erogenous zones, which happens when they feel calm and cosy. This is when, distracted, they seek the pleasant sensation of arousal. It doesn't lead to anything, except a few small signs of erection in boys, who may be enchanted by the intriguing manifestation, which may be treated positively or negatively by those around them. It is interesting to note that girls tend to stimulate their clitorises more regularly and often than boys play with their penises. Girls tend to entertain themselves for longer and with more intensity than boys do. They are rarely reprimanded for it nowadays, but in the past they were strongly discouraged from any kind of erotic practice such as masturbation. Centuries-old beliefs are not easy to undo and always leave traces of their presence in the minds of many people. People still ask me if masturbation can do any harm. To this day, parents don't know what to do when they find their daughter absorbed in a TV program stimulating herself erotically by repeatedly rubbing her clitoral region. Some girls do it at school too, and their teachers don't know what to do either, especially when it starts to affect their scholastic performance.

By the time they are 7 or 8, children are aware that sex is something very important in adult life. They know it isn't just any old subject and that they will also become enthused by it. **What they don't know is that this enthusiasm will be accompanied by sadness. Setbacks in this area are terrible, as they bring on dramatic feelings of humiliation – vanity's negative counterpart.** Acceptance is good for vanity, while rejection leads to feelings of humiliation. As we know, vanity first begins to express itself a little earlier, when children feel enormous pleasure exhibiting themselves after adorning their bodies with something (a pair of earrings, a necklace, special clothes, etc.).

Arousal takes place when the child adorns him or herself, but the biggest pleasure is in getting a show of approval – at times a little over-the-top – from the people around them. It is obvious that the child is seeking signs of admiration and that he has attributed value to it. The pleasures of vanity are very ephemeral, such that in order to repeat the feeling of gratification, successive adornments are required – the embryo of the consumerism that is so enticing to most people. **The insatiable, ephemeral nature of vanity, along with its omnipresence, is very well recorded in Ecclesiastes**[7].

[7] "Vanity of vanities, saith the Preacher, vanity of vanities; all is vanity." (Ecclesiastes 1:2)

Flávio Gikovate

Erotic exhibitionism usually takes place when boys and girls of about 8 or 9 are alone. Girls – and sometimes even boys – admire themselves in the mirror dressed up in their mother's or older sister's clothes and shoes. Boys imitate manly gestures like the ones they see in films or boys who have already reached puberty. They appear to be rehearsing what is to come and are aroused by their ideas of adult sexual life – always seen as very stimulating and fun.

The amount of information that boys and girls of this age have available to them nowadays is incomparable with that of previous generations. In the past, they learned about sexual matters in a veiled manner, shrouded in ignorance. They had heard of penetration, and boys, always isolated from girls, took turns trying to penetrate one another, usually without an erection, always very furtively, as if they were committing a crime. It is no wonder that, as adults, many remember these experiences with shame and guilt, and even doubt about their own manliness.

Boys' erotic games always used to involve a good dose of aggression, and I believe it remains true. Stronger boys used their strength to humiliate weaker ones, and such humiliation often had to do with erotic submission – diffuse and poorly formulated, since the bullies didn't know exactly what to do. The atmosphere, however, contained clear ingredients of the association between aggression and eroticism: uttering profanities, placing losers in submissive positions, taking off their clothes, among other practices which should have been repugnant, but caused many to laugh.

Things were always easier for girls. They masturbated a lot and continue to do so, with the significant difference that social tolerance has only grown – even when they stimulate themselves in public. In the past, everything with a touch of eroticism had to be done in private. Girls prepared for what would be expected of them as adults: they played with dolls, dollhouses, pretend cutlery sets, and so on. The atmosphere wasn't as competitive as it was in boys' games, which were always very separate to girls' games.

Boys didn't play with dolls (and don't often do so to this day), while girls didn't play football or do judo. Nowadays the frontiers between the male and female domains are coming undone, such that boys and girls play together much more. The content of these games, however, conforms to the male standard: competitive games, fights, all manner of competitions on the computer, etc. Girls are integrated into the male world, but the opposite isn't true. This is because the fear of stimulating homosexuality still haunts the vast majority of families with boys.

Erotic games between boys and girls also existed, but much less than those between boys, since they tended to be kept apart in their play.

Children have always exchanged caresses imitating what they think adults do. Mass communication produces more than enough information for them to know

Flávio Gikovate

every detail of adult sexual interaction nowadays. Before all this information was available, children were very perplexed if they saw their parents having sex.

Freud called this the "primal scene". It isn't hard to imagine the impact of such an image in the mind of a child in the past, much less informed than children today. Even when they didn't stay for the whole "show", they almost always heard some kind of noise coming from their parent's room. There is no doubt in my mind that such sights and sounds greatly reinforced the idea that sex and aggression were very united. Sexual intercourse, from a child's point of view, could only have been compared with a struggle, given the difficulties of distinguishing between moans of pleasure and pain.

What on earth could their parents be doing? Exchanging pleasurable caresses or beating each other up? If they watched all the way to the end, they'd have noticed a certain tenderness come over the couple, further increasing the perplexity and confusion in their tiny, fledgling minds, without enough information to decode what they'd seen. **Nowadays, would they be able to tell the difference between sex, the aggression that merely "spices up" sex, and tenderness? No matter how well informed they are, I don't think they are yet able to correctly interpret everything that takes place in their parents' sexual relations.**

I think that even children who have not witnessed a "primal scene" – whether between their parents or other adults with whom they have contact – are confused.

They may even have seen raunchy scenes on TV or in films, but nevertheless will be riddled with doubt about the ingredients that play a part in adult erotic intimacy and the right proportion of each – eroticism per se, aggression, tenderness – required for the best result. As such, I don't believe they really know what to expect of the future.

Later in childhood, many girls start becoming familiar with certain exaggerated aspects of female vanity, going with their mothers to beauty salons – not just to accompany them, but to get beauty treatments themselves. They become familiar with the characteristics of adult vanity and the artifices that can be used to improve their appearances in order to attract boys. Such practices, which seek to speed up the arrival of more traditional women's activities, are not terribly well thought-out, nor are they in keeping with women's new reality.

Boys tend to stay more focused on traditional competitive activities, perhaps trying to perfect sexist behaviour of a seductive nature, playing the "bad boy". It is a beginning with a bleak outlook for girls and boys, not to mention out-dated and conservative. We will see how things evolve in the years to come.

10. ten

It is hard not to compare what being a teenager was like fifty years ago with what it is like today. In many aspects, the changes have been big, truly radical. Unfortunately, we have advanced little in more essential aspects. I believe that the contradictions surrounding sex are more visible, which will usher in the substantial advances we need so badly in order to be happier. To cite just one example: when girls in the 1950s got their period, they felt very ashamed; sometimes they didn't even know what it was and thought they might have some kind of disease. Everything related to sex was shrouded in a dark, rather sinister fog. **Nothing seemed natural. It was as if "pure" creatures were being sullied, contaminated with impurities which – "unfortunately" – were a part of adult life.**

Nowadays, girls and boys wait anxiously for adult sex. It is as if a big party were to begin – fun, exciting and full of emotions, seen as among the most interesting things in life. Sex used to be a reason for shame; now it is something to be proud of. In the past, boys also bragged about quantitative abilities, both real and fictitious. They loved telling each other how many times they were able to ejaculate in a single night and how far their sperm flew when it happened. They compulsively measured their erect penises and then told their buddies their results – almost always amplified. Many lied, but they thought everyone else was telling the truth, which brought great feelings of inferiority regarding totally irrelevant aspects of male sexuality.

Shame, guilt and feelings of incompetence in sexual acts filled the minds of boys, whose first sexual experiences, almost always with prostitutes, were more like a competence test than something pleasurable. Young men and women lived in separate worlds and barely spoke to one another. They weren't friends; rather, they belonged to distinct "tribes" that were very interested in one another, but didn't have the slightest idea what the other was really like and what they thought. The only integrating factor was sight! Boys looked at girls with desire and girls looked at boys to see if they were being desired, which stirred the pleasant feeling of sexual arousal in them – reinforced by the pleasure of getting looks of admiration from observers, an erotic stimulus to one's vanity.

Being looked at by boys who were a better "catch" – according to the criteria of each group – gave girls more erotic pleasure of an exhibitionist nature than being looked at by men of an "inferior" social condition. On the other hand, boys have always looked at attractive girls regardless of their social standing. I believe this has changed very little and to this day indicates that men are far more visually stimulated than women. A woman may feel more inclined to accept a certain man's overtures if he has a pleasing physical appearance; however, his social standing and the role he plays in the group certainly influence his success or failure with her.

Men's physical appearance has undoubtedly grown as a social value, to such an extent that it may even seem that women experience visual desire too, previously repressed. This hypothesis is corroborated by the fact that nowadays many women take the initiative to approach men. However, as I have said before, I believe these changes are born of shifts in customs, rather than the result of the lifting of a form of repression. Most probably, since there are no longer such big differences separating the male and female worlds, women have gained access to the social and academic posts that they used to value so much in men. As a result, they can't admire men as much for glories that they themselves have also acquired. Male beauty, previously lower down on the list of priorities, has come to be more valued in this more homogenized world.

I would like to stress here – and emphatically – that beauty is an elitist property par excellence. That is, it is a quality that inevitably privileges only a small number of people of both sexes. By attributing enormous value to it, as is the case nowadays, society stimulates, more than in any other era, strong feelings of inferiority in the majority of people. This isn't, however, an inexorable fate of our heterogeneous species, in which attributes were not distributed equally. Different cultures may place greater or lesser value on certain characteristics – such as character virtues, discipline, the ability to establish quality relationships; a series of properties that are hard to obtain, but not impossible. In other words, the emotional happiness of some doesn't increase or reduce others' chances of success.

Nowadays, because beauty is a very important value, this is often one of the first negative blows that boys and girls experience in their early adolescence: they are not as good-looking as they would like to be! Highly frustrated, many become overly reserved. Others seek to counterbalance this disadvantage with their competence at sports, ability to make friends, sense of humour (considered very important, especially among boys) and, depending on the group, intellectual or artistic abilities, especially music. They seek to etch out a place for themselves in a world in which beauty seems to be fundamental.

Boys' main objective in this phase is to get physically close to the opposite sex. Girls want the same thing, even though they don't have the same strong desire that boys do. Visual desire isn't essential for them to want to get up close and personal with boys, touch them, feel the texture of their skin, and experience a real kiss, like the ones they see in films and on TV. This used to be a dream for 13-year-olds of both sexes of (who would only have their first kiss much later, when they had a proper girlfriend or boyfriend), but has become common practice since the 1990s. Teenagers invented this practice of "hooking up", and we only found out about it much later.

For the first time, at least in recent history, teenage boys and girls of the same social class and age group began to have erotic exchanges with no strings attached, without any knowledge of one another besides a quick chat at some noisy party. The boy desires the girl and she accepts him because his desire has aroused her. **They exchange limited caresses in the public place in which they met, which also means they must keep themselves in check, which allows them to get to know themselves sexually without being afraid. Getting to know one's own reactions is something new and essential for girls, who in the past used to be terrified of not being able to control their sexuality, seen as a dangerous dragon. This is no longer so, because they can learn to live with all, or almost all, of the details of female sexual arousal through these intimate encounters (in an atmosphere that isn't exactly romantic, but offers safety and quality).**

Because in the past boys only had physical contact with prostitutes or girls from much lower social classes, they had a twisted understanding of sexual practices. They didn't bother to get to know their partners, much less were they concerned if they had an orgasm or not – they didn't even know the characteristics of female pleasure. They were quantitative experiences, but which contributed little to any future quality relationship. As a result, although they thought they were very experienced, they were really little more so than girls. Nowadays, the number of boys interested in prostitutes is on the wane. For the first time, this profession appears to have gone into decline, as there are not enough replacements for the older men who now make up their client base.

Many teenage boys have sex for the first time with a girlfriend when they are about 16 or 17 years of age. They do so without any shame. This has also changed, because in the past their own fathers took it upon themselves to provide erotic opportunities to test their sons' manhood. This later initiation in an atmosphere of tenderness may be the beginning of a fundamental change in the quality of sexual relations and may even help break the strong link between sex and aggression. We owe all this to "hooking up". On the internet – where teenage boys find plenty of material for masturbation – sex and aggression are still strongly linked in the content of most erotic films and even interactive activities. This substitutes prostitutes and casual sex with girls of lower social classes, but it doesn't change the content of their fantasies. This is the midpoint in which we find ourselves at present, lighting a candle to God and another to the Devil.

The atmosphere of adolescence is thus heterogeneous. Some do well, especially the most insistent boys and the most attractive, sensual girls. Many don't do so well: those who don't have the courage to approach

girls because they don't feel good enough for them, or because they are afraid of being inconvenient or rejected; boys who are more modest, not so good-looking, less sociable or who do not fit the official standard of beauty. However, lack of success at this stage in life is not a precise indication of what is to come. There is a sense of optimism and hope visible on their faces, in their expansive gestures and easy laughter. Most are certain the future will be good to them. I hope it is.

The exchange of caresses involved in hooking up gives sex an atmosphere of naturalness, which is an important new achievement for our species. The practices are simple, naïve. They don't demand the ingredients of seduction, power games and attempts at emotional involvement. Some boys, and even girls, hook up with more than one partner at a single party. Many boys brag about it; while some girls are discreet or a little ashamed, for fear of being seen in a bad light.

Almost all of them masturbate: boys, stimulated by the abundance of pornographic material available; girls, imagining erotic situations of an exhibitionist nature or even more romantic encounters. Elements of aggression are present in most of the erotic material aimed at men. Most girls, who obviously have access to these sites too, are less interested in them than boys are, as the aggressive elements associated with sexuality aren't present in all women. **Those who develop more aggression are those who grew up with penis envy, now thirsty for revenge, as they have discovered that women and girls**

are not the fragile sex. This is true today more than ever. They can use their sexual advantage to humiliate: leading boys on, but not allowing them to get too close.

I reiterate my belief that penis envy is something that will soon be a thing of the past. This is another important positive variable on the horizon. Boys and girls grow up in much closer contact, play the same sports, study together, and so on. It didn't used to be so. There has also been a radical change during adolescence, in which parents' fear of their daughters sexual activity has lessened considerably since the advent of the contraceptive pill. Additionally, women are occupying more and more space in all areas of adult activity. As a result, there is no more reason for this element of hostility toward men to persist in children or adults. Women who grew up to be immature, unable to tolerate frustrations and obstacles, will have to find another way to give vent to their frustrations. They will no longer be able to blame their husbands for the fact that they don't work or think they are being held back professionally or socially just because they are women.

They will be able, if they wish, to continue sexually provoking men, however, I believe they will be increasingly unsuccessful, due to the interesting phenomena taking place with younger men. They still have visual desire for women. But it doesn't mean they chase after them as they used to. They seem to have discovered something extraordinarily liberating: that desire is good to feel, but they do not have to be ruled by it!

Flávio Gikovate

This is, perhaps, one of the deepest blows to sexism. Once again we owe this innovation to 16 and 17-year-olds who changed their standard behaviour without consulting us. Because this phenomenon began to emerge about fifteen years ago, many of them are already older. The fact is that they are calmer and not in such a hurry to get close to real girls. They entertain themselves with the virtual world and don't feel the traditional macho obligation to constantly chase after women and never miss an opportunity to approach them. They are fine on their own. This "calm" is also reflected in their application to their studies and their future professional life. It is as if everything were related – and it really used to be, at least for men. Women now work and make their own living, which takes the pressure off them to be providers. If men aren't well accepted by them it isn't a problem, because they entertain themselves with virtual women, who are just as or more interesting. It has always been women who were in a hurry to get married and have children. Men have, perhaps, become a little more complacent than is ideal. Nevertheless, this appears to be a new male tendency in the face of women's advances.

The fact is that from primitive times to this day women have always been the winners in the so-called "war of the sexes." Before that, they were definitely the weaker ones, both in terms of sexual advances and in satisfying their survival needs. **Nowadays they are sexually free, which means they only have sexual contact**

Flávio Gikovate

when and with whom they want to. They are financially independent and don't need providers. They can decide if they want to have children or not and if they want to get married and have a stable partner or not. I still don't think they are fully aware of their wonderful achievement and the privileged condition they have built for themselves over the millenniums that separate us from our pre-history. It is impossible for men not to be perplexed and paralyzed in the face of such radical changes.

eleven

I hope I am being clear and convincing in my efforts to show how hard it is to reflect on sexuality in the decades following the 1960s, when things began changing at a frightening speed. This was, at least in part, due to other changes – the consequence of an uninterrupted string of technological advances. I do not underestimate the strength and determination of the first feminists, much less the influence they had on a large contingent of women, especially younger ones.

The second half of the 1960s saw a very special atmosphere arise in the existential lives of young people. The process had already been set in motion in the late 1950s, with the arrival of rock-n-roll music, particularly due to the widespread influence of Elvis Presley. Because of him, men earned the right to dance extravagantly and even sway their hips. With his music, couples stopped dancing as pairs – with the woman always being led by the man – and people started dancing in their own way, although still facing one another and united by looks of togetherness or steps that required them to hold hands. This is more relevant than it might appear at first sight: this was when pairs became un-

paired, even if not entirely. It marked the beginning of the reign of individuality, which came to be just as or more important than love.

The 1960s were set to music with mastery by bands such as the Beatles and the Rolling Stones, to cite only a few of the most popular ones. There was an atmosphere of sexual freedom – always facilitated by the presence of drugs, especially marijuana, which helped more conservative young men and women adhere to the new order. There were also strong anti-war sentiments, especially with regards to the disastrous Vietnam War. The era was marked by thinkers such as Herbert Marcuse, spokesman for an important tendency (which arose in Germany and was exported to the United States before World War II) that reconciled the thinking of Marx and Freud. In keeping with this point of view, it was believed that sexual liberation – understood as the end of possessive, monogamous alliances between couples – would create an atmosphere of less frustration and competition, compatible with a fairer social order.

The ideas were beautiful and the intentions formidable. But it's always the same old story: theory must be put to the test to see how it works in practice. Feminism and women's newfound sexual freedom – as a result of their growing economic independence and the advent of the contraceptive pill – gave them the legitimate right to use their bodies as they pleased. They grew bolder about displaying them and became even more attractive to men. Attitudes stemming from men's long-standing envy of women's sensual power were also exacerbated: I saw aggressive demonstrations by men who were angry at the girls who went topless on Rio de Janeiro's famous beaches. Most men were more discreet and subtle in their protests, however, since few had the courage to speak out against the social tendency of the era.

At first, these more daring women, companions in drug-use and sexually attractive, were drawn to hippies; that is, sensitive, slender men, bold in their more effeminate dress code (sandals, man-bags, Indian-style cotton shirts), interested in artistic activities and almost never very financially successful. They made their living as artisans, selling photographs, busking in public places. In reality, they got by with the help of their families, as they came from the upper and middle classes and their parents financed their studies (and hoped their offspring were merely going through a strange, but fleeting phase).

Responsible, committed relationships seemed to have gone out of fashion for these irreverent young men and women, who wanted more out of life than tedious traditional marriages. They experimented with life in communities in which sexual freedom was supposed to be the highest value; that is, there were no set couples or rights over one another. The end of jealousy had been decreed. It didn't work exactly as hoped,

Flávio Gikovate

since the women had their preferences and weren't always equally available to all members of the group. The men pretended not to be bothered by the occasional rejection, made easier by the use of drugs, which attenuated all forms of psychological pain. They pretended not to be bothered, but they were, of course, and maybe would even avenge themselves at a later date.

Things moved along in fits and starts, but conflicts were easily resolved due to the indolence brought on by marijuana. But, suddenly, a particular pair would fall in love for real and jealously – which isn't resolved by decree – would raise its head, and the desire for exclusivity would prevail over the libertarian ideals that had been placed on a pedestal and discussed at such length. **It was love imposing its conservative norms and demands. Apparently, sex was liberation and love was the villain that ended up leading people to matrimony and the end of freedom. The passing years have clarified this issue.**

Successful young men were, thus, those who followed the commandments of idleness, competent at sunbathing and enjoying life under the effect of drugs.[8] More serious, hard-working young men were only attractive to the girls who hadn't adhered to the hippie

---

[8] Previous generations had been brought up in an atmosphere of obligation and duty, and were totally unprepared for an idle, frivolous lifestyle, which they felt was unbearable. I believe that drugs helped create the psychological conditions for a life without responsibilities, for which young people weren't prepared.

movement, who, in turn, were less exhibitionist and apparently less interesting. An exception was the small number of young people who adhered to egalitarian political movements. They occupied an intermediate space between the hippies and more traditional types, and also had their admirers, fascinated by the epic, heroic nature of their intentions. Many died. Others went into political life and didn't always honour their ideals.

In the 1970s, the Beatles split up, signalling the end of dreams. Young hippies became almost irremediable drug-addicts or went back to university and sought to reintegrate in more traditional lifestyles. Besides blue jeans, little was left of their libertarian ideals. The exhibitionism of many women didn't recoil with these changes, however, and continued to grow. While previously they had been attracted to non-materialistic, radical hippie types, with time their interest shifted back to men who sought careers and a good social and financial standing. But this didn't stop them from advancing professionally and socially, increasingly investing in studies and credentials in order to become independent. Men, on the other hand, reverted to traditional standards.

In the 1960s, the hippie movement saw a closing of the gap between male and female behaviour, in dress codes and long hair as well as sensitivity. Men also started doing the domestic activities traditionally assigned to women, previously off-limits to men, who were supposed to honour their manhood. This created an optimistic perspective in which men and women came closer together, reducing the gender gap. By the early 1980s, things had reverted to the way they were before: men had returned to their traditional standards, as if they hadn't adapted so well to the new way of life they had created. **Women, in turn, started wearing ties and the clothes they wore looked a lot like men's. It was a clear sign of their professional and social advancement, now seeking equality within male standards. On the beaches, however, their bathing suits kept shrinking.**

It's not impossible that this return to the male standard, now a reference for both genders, has also been influenced by the growing number of attractive and interesting new goods available on the market, capable of making most people want to own them. Many of these material goods don't have anything to do – at least not at first – with the erotic game of seduction. That is, it isn't always female adornments or male objects that spark interest. It is electronics: cell phones, computers, DVDs, and a whole host of other products that enchant us. **Consumerism has a new face, now not only related to eroticism. Objects are becoming attractive in themselves. There is more competition, but not necessarily only for the purpose of gaining access to the opposite sex.**

I have observed that, starting in the 1990s, both women's and men's lives have acquired a complexity that still requires a great deal of reflection by those

who wish to understand their current reality. Some women have advanced in the professional world, which is becoming more and more socially relevant. They are expected to exhibit more male behaviour, and those who don't hold well-paid jobs feel inferior. Some aren't drawn to the competitive professional world and prefer to marry and occupy themselves with respectable and complex domestic activities (though their prestige is undermined by the modern code that holds professional work as the utmost value). Others have sought to make the most of their privileged physical appearance to find partners and, through them, move up the social ladder and acquire the means to attain their material dreams.

Men have also been living through complicated times, since most still try to find a place in the professional world and now face growing competition with women, who are increasingly well-qualified. Many marry women who also have jobs, and find themselves in unexpected situations, such as losing their job and having to be supported by their wife or dealing with the fact that the wife is more successful. Many couples are unable to cope with this reality and end up divorcing. Younger men don't even feel apt to compete with women, who are increasingly active and entrepreneurial. These men are passive and don't even consider getting married as they don't believe they are capable of dealing with the responsibilities that come with such a commitment. They are waiting to

see what lies ahead for them. We also need to wait and see!

I think one inheritance of the 1960s, besides blue jeans, is the idea that sex is the most relevant thing in life. As such, the men who are most successful with women are the ones who are most envied by their peers, even when we know they are of dubious character, liars, etc. Players are male role models and those who aren't envy them. Look at the paradox: the best envy the worst. The best men are more respectful, more concerned with women's feelings, and try not to frustrate them by making promises they can't keep. They are also the ones who are most afraid of becoming emotionally involved. Players don't run the risk of becoming involved and, perhaps for this very reason, find it easy to approach even the most attractive women.

Female beauty and sensuality are growing in importance and even the most intelligent, productive women dream of looking like those who spend the whole day preening themselves so as to be more seductive. This inflation of the importance of sex, including casual sex, has only brought suffering and discomfort to an enormous number of people, including those who are successful in the area and those who aren't. Rivalry and competition between women have grown, also extending into their professional lives. It is curious, but nowadays they seem to try to have it all in order to enchant and seduce the greatest possible number of men.

Men, in turn, regard them with mistrust, and many of the best feel that they are out of their league; as a result, they don't even approach them. Players are becoming more and more competent in the art of seduction and (due to the envious hostility they have always harboured for women) take pleasure in building up hopes that will never be realized. They approach the more attractive ones with greater ease and many marry them with explicitly opportunistic objectives.

We have, on the one hand, men who cultivate hostility. On the other, men who feel intimidated. We also have apathetic, disinterested youths. Few feel calm and collected about approaching women. Casual sex is only of interest to the first group. Members of the second group wish they had the courage to approach nice women and establish emotional ties with them. And youths, as I said, still don't know what they want.

As for women, there are those who love to exhibit themselves and incite desire in the most coveted men, perhaps with less hostility than before. And there are women who would love to do the same, but don't feel physically competent for it. There are women who are aware that they can't use their physical beauty to attract men of their own generation and decide to focus on older men, who are still fascinated by their beauty. And women who are increasingly aware that they will have to be financially self-sufficient, because men no longer earn enough to maintain traditional standards and support a family with their work alone, and also because they can't rule out the possibility that they might not get married.

People are increasingly fascinated with the consumption of personal items and technological goods. They try their hardest to impress members of the opposite sex, at the same time as they have to show everyone, men and women, that they are professionally and financially successful. They spend more and more time alone (the divorce rate has also grown a lot) and they usually aren't prepared for it. They think a lot about sex, and when they practice it, they do what they have learned watching x-rated films, which isn't always terribly satisfying. Both men and women dream of beauty and superfluous material goods. Depression is widespread. Men and women don't understand each other. Friendships are fluid and the quality of emotional ties isn't growing. The legacy of these years is not brilliant.

twelve

This is more or less where we are at now. The outlook isn't encouraging, but despair is not part of the history of our species. Nor is easy, quick, radical change. We should be wary of the efficiency of large-scale movements, though they allow us to understand things that were previously hard to observe. It is up to us to sort the wheat from the chaff and look for springboards for small advances, which are always possible. I am thinking of individual advances and believe that collective advances depend on the individual adhesion of a good number of people.

I have been systematically studying romantic relationships since the 1970s. I used to be convinced it wouldn't take people long to see the interpersonal poverty of casual erotic relationships and re-focus on quality emotional involvements. Affinity between the sexes has grown, since they spend more time together as children and lead more similar adult lives. I believed that character affinities would end up proving very relevant in the choice of romantic partners. I imagined that relationships would become more solid, intense and stable. I believed in this because I knew that love was still something most people longed for. **I thought that the reign of sex – and its association with aggressiveness – was running out of steam, coming to an end.**

It seems that once again I was mistaken. I don't believe I was wrong about what would happen, as dissatisfaction and depression are widespread and one day people will want a better solution than the use of antidepressants – which, curiously, have a considerable impact on sexual function! But I was mistaken about the speed with which these changes would take place (although I continue to believe in them). **We are impatient beings and want people to notice our good ideas quickly, which leads us to assume that common sense will soon prevail. However, society as a whole progresses more slowly. Crowds are slower than individuals.**

What do we see nowadays? Men and women who are unable to establish loving relationships based on affinities, which means that relationships between opposites – those who attract one another but don't work well together – are still more common. People speak of "soul mates", but still go looking for their "better half". They establish weak relationships, largely mismatched and replete with repetitive arguments. They frequently marry their opposites, and divorce almost as often. Some stop believing in love and slot into the current norm of looking for partners for casual sex, in which the commitment – when there is one – is superficial. Others learn to live better alone and hope to find a more consistent loving relationship than the last one. Sometimes, out of impatience, they make mistakes and become involved with people with whom they don't have any real affinities, and are disappointed once again. Others seek to fill their lives with friendships, work, electronic games and, not infrequently, virtual relationships through the internet. A few give up on interpersonal relationships for good and start living for individual pleasures. The path that each person takes depends on many factors, including the age at which they find that their relationship – of dubious quality – is over.

Cultural pressure, as we know, stops us from enjoying our current so-called sexual freedom to the fullest. Sex is seen as a pleasure par excellence, and most of the products consumed are for personal improvements aimed at better results in the search for sexual partners. People, especially women, will often spend much of their time and money on improving their physical appearance. Men also groom themselves more and more, as they prepare to frequent places where little talking and a lot of looking goes on. They also try, of course, to display signs of their socioeconomic condition, now also important for women, because men are no longer expected to be sole providers.

Encounters are superficial and people say little about what they really think and feel. They quickly pair up, like teenagers, except that they also hop into bed together. A few hours later they are lying on a bed or a sofa at one of their houses. The sex has the typi-

Flávio Gikovate

cal aspects of a first encounter: a certain embarrassment at being nude in front of the other person (no matter how well they look after themselves, they always have some imperfection that they fear will be discovered and reduce the admiration that they want to incite), followed by a great deal of concern about their performance. At the same time that they must show they are competent, they don't always feel comfortable enough for less traditional practices. Everyone feels awkward and unsure as to how to behave. And to top it off there is the renewed male preoccupation with penis size – because of porno films that use "well hung" men – and the ability to maintain an erection for a long period of time and perhaps even have sex several times in one night.

Everyone is concerned with themselves and the impression they are going to give their casual partner. They also worry about what that person might say to third parties, as they almost always have acquaintances in common. They really worry about it. It is dubious as to whether they are interacting with one another in a real and deep way. They exchange caresses, but both are thinking about themselves, aiming for a good result that will prop up their vanity. Even the act of pleasing one's partner has personal objectives: we like to know that the other person is aroused by what we do to them, since we are aroused by their arousal. In other words, the only thing that matters is knowing if we are pleasing them.

Flávio Gikovate

It's impossible not to believe that the interpersonal ingredients here are minimal and secondary. They use one another to achieve personal objectives of arousal, self-affirmation, ejaculation and orgasm. What happens after men have ejaculated, however, demonstrates even more clearly the extent to which the other person is irrelevant; they want to get out of there as fast as they can. Often, in an effort to keep up appearances and be polite, they behave subtly, but it isn't always possible. Women are more comfortable because their orgasms, when they happen, don't bring on the same feeling of satiation that ejaculation does. There is a residual excitement that allows them to remain interested in a casual partner. However, they are disappointed and hurt when they realise the feeling isn't reciprocal and that the man's interest was "purely sexual".

Even when they know this is the case, it seems that women always hope to enchant their partners enough so they won't want to be merely casual. In other words, it is as if, deep down, they long to be able to awaken something more than sexual desire, which is a victory for them. They experience this feeling of victory even when they are not really interested in that particular man: he should feel totally enchanted and fascinated to the extent that he never wants to let her out of his sight again. It would be the full realization of her sensual power, which, unfortunately for her, disappears as soon as the man ejaculates.

Victory for men is managing to get a woman into bed; for women, it is for the man to want to see them

Flávio Gikovate

again after that casual encounter. This is the dispute, and the final result almost always favours men. The women wait for the phone to ring in the days after the event, not so much because they really enjoyed that particular partner, but because it would mean that the encounter made an impression and was unforgettable – which is music to their vanity. The men, who are well aware of this, almost never call, thereby avenging themselves of the effort of convincing the women to go out with them in the first place.

What I have just described is strongly contaminated by aggression. There is no tenderness, pleasure in one another's company, no trace of any kind of intimate human contact. Things couldn't be any different, because intimacy requires hours of conversation, at least minimal knowledge of each other's life history, a liking for the other person's behaviour. Based on this, there may be genuine pleasure in pleasing the other – which, of course, depends on knowing what they do and don't like. What appears to have some interpersonal motivation is nothing more than the manifestation of vanity: pleasing the other person in order to feel good, strong and superior.

This is a clear example of the presence of aggression and absolute disinterest in whether or not their partner will be upset if they don't take things any further. Men vanish from women's lives after one-night stands and are even pleased when they hear they were upset, hoping they'd at least show them a little friendliness – by phoning, sending flowers, etc. Women go about making themselves even more attractive and may learn to be firmer and not to give in to sexual pressure so quickly. They will try to develop more sophisticated strategies so they won't be subjected to the same humiliation after sexual encounters. They may even think about playing it up during sex, pretending to feel more pleasure and explicitly imitating the porn actresses who have taught us everything. Interestingly, in these films the scenes also end when the men ejaculate!

The truth is that, as far as casual sex is concerned, men almost always win. They have the advantage of the refractory period, in which they no longer feel any kind of sexual desire. At this moment, they look at their partners with objectivity rather than desire. Few are the women who pass the test of remaining interesting from this point on (as this would imply pleasures of another nature, which have to do with really getting to know them). **Few women truly enjoy such encounters; and even those who derive a reasonable amount of pleasure from the experience are not usually fine about men's traditional lack of consideration afterwards.** Most end up thinking that it isn't worth it and that the moments of pleasure don't make up for the upsets afterwards. They give up on casual sex, which, in my opinion, really doesn't have a big future.

I have already said that the best men, the ones who are saddened when they make others suffer, are less skilled at this kind of erotic game, in which someone always gets hurt. It is disappointing to see that the nicest men are envious of the most callous precisely because they are successful at something that is highly valued; finding partners for casual sex. More reserved women may also feel envious of less discreet ones because of the looks of desire they elicit. Maybe one day people will wake up to the fact that the fun and charm of these casual encounters is grossly overrated, and maybe this will improve the self-esteem of those who don't feel comfortable with them.

13
thirteen

It is important to note here that the individuals considered the most sensual are precisely those who look for casual sex, who are better at the erotic game of seduction and not terribly trustworthy. In other words, more honest, sincere and loving people end up being seen as not very attractive, as they don't stir insecurity or doubt in others. It is sad to note that the people generally seen as sensual tend to be those of dubious character. **Everything seems to suggest that sensuality derives, among other ingredients, from the challenge – the feeling that someone is hard to seduce and will always slip through our fingers. That is, sensuality springs from the perception that the person won't let down their guard, that they will always be a challenge.**

According to this way of thinking, someone who truly loves is not very sensual in the eyes of their beloved! What a sad example for young people, hungry for satisfying sexual experiences and quality romantic relationships. Looking around, they learn that they will have to make a terrible choice between being loving (and not so attractive) or being rude, aggressive and untrustworthy (and thus sexually interesting).

Based on these observations, we can raise some important points about the role of sex in choosing and maintaining emotional involvements. I have written a lot about the obstacles faced by those who wish to establish good-quality loving relationships[9].. When two people have strong affinities, they tend to form intense bonds, which can be very threatening to the individuality of those who are trying to become emotionally involved. They feel bad when they realise that they are "losing themselves" in the other person, which they don't want. This is very frightening, and couples experience what is called "falling in love": a feeling of affinity and "fitting together" romantically, accompanied by an equal amount of fear.

I have also written about the fear we all have of suffering over a break-up. We fear it even when we have had no previous experience of the sort, since our first connection to someone (our symbiosis with our mother while in the womb) ended in this manner – and with indescribable suffering. I have written several times about the fear of happiness that grips us when we feel complete and in harmony as a result of a fully satisfying romantic encounter. It is as if it were the announcement of imminent tragedy, of something horrible that is going to happen – as if happiness provoked the wrath of the gods and the envy of other humans. The truth of the matter is that we don't know

---

[9] See my books on the subject, especially *A Love Story... with a Happy Ending.*

how to deal with so much harmony, because our conditioning tells us that it can't end well (also related to our symbiosis in the womb that ended tragically with our dramatic expulsion and the painful act of being born). In my opinion, this experience lies at the root of all of our superstitions. The fear is particularly strong in matters of love due to their similarity to our childhood experience and the intense happiness we feel when we find someone with whom we share a great deal of affinity.

These reasons, together with the low self-esteem that affects most of us (especially in our youth) and causes us not to admire people who are similar to us, are more than enough to undermine any enchantment, even between people who are different enough not to have to fear losing themselves in one another. Another powerful ingredient is still missing in this complex, disastrous scenario. Sexual desire takes up a very malignant position, usually during youth, when its potency should not be underestimated.

Young people know what I'm talking about as they usually have a few members of the opposite sex among their close friends. Sincere, true friends are those with whom they share the same dreams and ideals and feel comfortable enough to talk freely without fear of being judged or censured. **It is curious that, considering their degree of intimacy and the quality of their contact, no sign of sexual desire ap-**

Flávio Gikovate

pears – for many years, at least[10]. Friendship is characterized by reciprocal trust and certainty of loyalty. The hurt caused by a friend's disloyalty is almost as great as that of a relationship break-up.

It is evident that sexual desire is fuelled by everything that is not present in friendships: mistrust, different behaviour patterns and ways of thinking that make it harder to understand exactly how the other person's mind works, in addition to strong character differences. I have written countless times that we can identify two basic types of people[11]: more selfish sorts, who can lie easily, don't feel guilt, are good at acting on their own behalf (even if this is aggressive or harmful to others), extroverted and superficial in conversation; and more generous sorts, whose overactive sense of guilt leads them to say "yes" when they'd like to say "no", and who are too docile, excessively dedicated to their partners and don't worry about reciprocity. They want to please their partners and be loved – even if it means renouncing their own rights.

The most sexually attractive human beings are selfish sorts, those who are unable to tolerate frustration and

---

10 This rule can, obviously, fail at some point in a close friendship and one of the friends may become sexually interested in the other. At this point, and only then, it occurs to them that the intense friendship was a neighbour of love and that the erotic ingredient is an unequivocal indication of it. The phenomenon is almost always unilateral, which is a shame, because when it is reciprocal it gives rise precisely to one of those rare loving relationships of excellent quality – that occur with some frequency in the early years of adult life.

11 See my book *Evil, Good and Beyond*.

setbacks. This means that if they have a desire that exceeds the limits of their romantic bond they don't think twice about fulfilling it. It is impossible to trust them, because they lie and are good with words: they make accusations to defend themselves, change the facts, threaten and cheat. They are not reliable, and for this reason are always very interesting, because it is as if they must be re-seduced every step of the way. They are like a bar of wet soap, slipping through your hands all the time.

I don't think this is the only ingredient of human sensuality; however, it shouldn't be underestimated. Physical appearance, a person's behaviour and facial expressions, the intensity of their sexual instinct and the clarity with which they affirm their desire (which varies from person to person) also count, in addition to other unknown factors. However, the figure of the player – and his female equivalent, the temptress, who dresses and acts provocatively – is undoubtedly more attractive than the figure of the nice man (sometimes overly respectful and polite) or the discreet woman!

It is interesting to note that, from a strictly sexual point of view, more selfish – less trustworthy – men and women also prefer selfish partners. In other words, more generous women are more fascinated by players, just as more selfish women are. Neither sort is particularly drawn to more generous men, which frustrates and saddens the latter. Generous men are fascinated by women who are seductive and exhibi-

tionists, just as more selfish men are. More modest, serious women, even beautiful ones, elicit less sexual interest. However, when choosing romantic partners, something different takes place. More selfish sorts prefer – not for sexual or romantic, but practical reasons – generous partners, who are more dependable and devoted. More generous sorts are still fascinated and establish relationships with selfish sorts, even if it goes against their practical interests.

The selfish don't establish strong ties with partners who are equally as selfish as they are because they can't trust them at all. They know from their own experience that they won't be able to resist the temptations of day-to-day life. Additionally, both tend to be very aggressive, so the intensity and violence of their fights – not infrequently physical – also make being together unviable. The generous could easily live alongside other generous sorts, but this tends to be rare due to the reasons I described earlier, in addition to a further ingredient: more generous men often don't feel as sexually competent when they are with a partner who makes them feel safe, awakens feelings of tenderness, doesn't give them reasons to fight, and doesn't stimulate their aggressive side.

When faced with these facts, it is easy to see why good relationships are so rare. It is also easy to appreciate how hard it is for sex not to be an important part of these competitive factors, in the context of a culture that treats the game of seduction (which contains obvious aggressive ingredients, because most of the time someone gets hurt) as an aphrodisiac. Men and women who are less skilled at (or willing to) put themselves first find they never have the upper hand. They almost always feel frustrated. They don't understand the situation, much less how their behaviour also ends up undermining their relationships.

This is all very sad, and we urgently need to decode the many variables involved in this intricate process that benefits the most emotionally immature and overlooks the rights of those around them, at least in youth. The envy that the generous tend to develop towards the selfish almost always originates precisely in the "advantage" that they have in sexual and emotional matters. More selfish types are loved by their generous partners. They are treated with great affection but are not reciprocal in their treatment: they like to be loved, but never surrender to the feeling themselves – for fear of suffering and also because they realize that much of their power comes from not showing the signs of trustworthiness that those who are truly involved show.

I have written several times about sexual intimacy in the most common type of stable relationship (between a selfish and a generous person), and I will briefly repeat myself here: a selfish man will have an exciting sex life with his generous wife because when he gets to know her better he'll discover that she is very sensual. Generous men, however, are almost always married to selfish wives, who are not good sex partners and generally avoid giving their best even in this aspect of life. They may also hold back in this area due to the envy and hostility they develop towards their generous partner. Couples where both are selfish tend to have an intense sex life, fight a lot and often break up after a short period of time. Couples where both are generous are also few and far between, and their sex lives tend to be good, but less intense. Men experience significant difficulties in the early days of these relationships, while women don't have the same problems.

It would appear that more selfish women act like men, from a sexual point of view. That is, their behaviour is strongly influenced by elements that are as competitive as they are aggressive. The sexuality of more generous ones is less subject to these factors and they find it easier to love. Selfish women do better in the context of casual sex, where aggression comes into play. Generous women don't fare so well with casual sex precisely because they don't know how to say "no", much less do they want to lead someone on and then reject them. They usually seek and prefer stable relationships and, after having been let down by a certain number of players, have a hard time finding partners: selfish men no longer interest them and generous men are drawn to temptresses or are still not ready for intense ties. The situation for men isn't much better: after a few disappointments, they are no longer interested in selfish women but still lack the courage to be with the ones with whom they could truly be happy (among other reasons, because they don't feel the same sexual desire for them). We need to find our way out of this labyrinth as quickly as possible!

fourteen

I think this is an appropriate moment to pose some considerations about male homosexuality. It is a thorny subject for those who are not content just taking on board the "official" thinking. Nowadays homosexuality is said to be an innate characteristic. Or, contradictorily, people sometimes talk about it as a choice. I will try to present here some reflections that appear to make sense in the light of what I have observed in my clinical experience. It is not my intention to refute other points of view; I only wish to state my own openly and free of prejudice or dogma.

I don't rule out the possibility that there may be certain innate components that lead to male homosexuality[12]**. The first and most evident is connected to physical appearance: it is common knowledge that some of the handsomest men are homosexual.** This frequency, well outside of statistical probabilities in my opinion, suggests that we are looking at a relevant fact in need of a coherent hypothesis. We cannot just be surprised by a fact of this magnitude and fail to include it among the complex

---

12 Note that what is true for men isn't always true for women. Female homosexuality requires its own chapter, located later in the book.

variables that influence the development of homosexuality. I have met people perplexed by this fact on countless occasions, but I have never heard anyone try to establish a correlation between it and homosexual behaviour.

Other innate factors related to appearance may also have some influence (not as striking as physical beauty). This is the case of heavier boys who, from an early age, have wider hips or more protruding breasts than most. They may be the object of teasing and humiliation as a result, which, as we will see, tends to interfere negatively in traditional male identity construction. They may suspect that they have more feminine characteristics due to an excess of female hormones and, even if it isn't true, may be influenced by this kind of idea.

Another element that, in my view, has to do with our innate characteristics is our ability to act and react more aggressively, along with the intensity of our fears. I believe that we are born different in many ways, among which if we tend to be fearless or easily scared. Our competence for aggression may be related to the intensity of our fear and may also contain personal ingredients. As such, there are boys who are more aggressive and not very fearful (who fit our culture's standard of virility), just as there are boys who are not very aggressive and who are very fearful. They are called names like "poof" or "pansy" from 4 or 5 years of age, a period in which socialization among children becomes more important.

There are also people who are very aggressive and not very fearful who, if they are also intelligent, may use their intellectual potential to throw powerful darts at their adversaries. Their behaviour will not be very violent, but some of the things they say (and even their sense of humour) show that their subjectivity is rich in hostility. The ingestion of alcohol and the use of other drugs can also free up their contained hostility.

I think it is interesting to note the large number of gay men dedicated to all kinds of artistic pursuits. It is hard to tell if there is a relationship between the innate presence of specific gifts for music, dance, set design, the fine arts, etc. and homosexuality. It is quite possible that the greatest influence is cultural in nature, given that many families don't encourage their boys to take up artistic pursuits.

As regards societal influence, I would like to stress, first and foremost, that there is a world of typically male behaviour and another of typically female behaviour. This has changed a lot since the end of the 20th century, but in family life there are still activities considered more masculine (related to the use of machines and cars) and others considered more feminine (concerned with domestic chores). As a rule, women decorate themselves more than men do, use more cosmetics and look after their hair more regularly. Men tend to be more interested in TV sports shows, while women prefer films, and so on. **In other words, in spite of a growing tendency for men's and women's behavioural standards to blur, there are still gender-assigned behaviours that are culturally attributed to each sex.** As I have said previously, there is the female sex and the practices that define the gender. In the same manner, there is the male sex and its corresponding gender.

Each boy and girl will realize, perhaps at the end of the second year of life, that they belong to one sex or the other. There will be those with penises and those without them. **When I think about what goes on in the minds of children when they discover that there are two different "types" of human beings, I imagine it must be a big shock to them and that they are surprised by this unexpected observation.** Boys realize that they are like their fathers, and girls recognise themselves as belonging to the same group as their mothers.

It should be pointed out that, at this age, each child already has his or her own embryo of "software". By the age of 3 children already "know" a lot about themselves and the world around them. They already have food, toy, and TV show preferences, and many may prefer the personality and behaviour of one parent, one grandparent, or even other adults. **In discussions of the duality between biology and culture, children's subjectivity – the way they feel and decode the things they learn – is almost always overlooked or neglected**[13].

---

[13] We cannot continue to make this fundamental mistake, which is still common due to the fact that, with the passing years, the particular way each child sees the world tends to be increasingly standardised due to the growing influence of culture on our way of thinking. That is, as children (and even teenagers), we form an identity and our own way of thinking; as we become adults, we tend to adapt to official cultural standards. It is a shame, because it greatly reduces the diversity that could exist among us thanks to the fact that, at our origin, our "hardware" and "software" are unique.

Flávio Gikovate

We cannot write off the possibility that a boy of this age likes his mother more than his father and is more drawn to her personality. We cannot dismiss the possibility that he might rebel against the gendered-behaviours of his own sex and decide to imitate the behaviour of his mother and other women. Despite being of the male sex, he may identify with female gender traits: he may be interested in dolls, domestic activities, beauty products and even typically women's clothes. **In the future, he will have memories that connect him with the female gender as far back as he can remember, which makes him suppose that he was born that way. He doesn't realize that the phenomenon of identifying with the female gender may come from the way he decoded the environment around him at a tender age.**

Boys like the one described above grow up with clearly effeminate behaviour from the outset and it isn't uncommon for them to seek a female body for themselves, one that is compatible with the gender they feel they belong to. This is the path taken by transvestites and those who undergo radical surgery to adapt their bodies to the mind they have developed. These phenomena are complex and still require a great deal of sincerely unbiased reflection on the part of those who study them. At any rate, I reaffirm that we cannot just continue to gaze at these facts in perplexity without paying attention to their details. It doesn't make any sense to consider them either abominable or completely natural. I don't think they are either.

Flávio Gikovate

It may be harder for boys with more curves (typical of the female body) to integrate with the male gender, just as it may also be harder for the very good-looking ones, who are admired for their looks – an experience that is more common, in our culture, with women. These facts do not provoke such inevitable and radical movements as the identification with the female gender that occurs in earlier phases of life, as some boys won't be teased about their bodies until they are around 7 years of age, by which time they already have many other inner defences. They will be more vulnerable if, in addition to more feminine bodies, they are also adverse to sports or attracted, for example, to dance – which, in our culture, is a typically female interest. They will also suffer if they do not know how to defend themselves, sometimes even physically; that is, if they are less aggressive or afraid of getting beaten up and hitting others.

From 6 to 12 or 13 years of age, the standard of virility in a culture like ours is clearly defined. Among the main ingredients that characterise the rough-cut macho man that they all try hard to be: boys have to be competent in disputes that involve physical fighting; they have to show an interest in the sporting activities popular in their peer group of reference; they must not be attracted by the kind of talk and activities seen as the domain of women. Those who find it hard to adapt become the brunt of sarcasm and jokes and are treated as if they are less manly and destined to a typically homosexual adult life. They are constantly humiliated and don't believe they have the strength to stand up for themselves. **Their parents tell them everything they don't want to hear: that they should fight back, avenge themselves of the aggressions they suffer. They are advised to act in precisely the manner that they are unable to, which reinforces even further their inner feeling of incompetence.**

Parents worry a lot about the sexual future of their more sensitive sons, those who don't integrate with other boys at school, in the street or the neighbourhood. They worry even more if they are introspective, interested in cultural or artistic pursuits. The situation worsens if their sons like the company of girls, or – worse – take an interest in their activities. Believing that this kind of identification will be fatal to their sons' sexual future, their parents try to impose rough, unattractive activities on them, making them even more resentful.

These sensitive, non-aggressive, more fearful boys suffer almost constant humiliation from their colleagues. They are also frequently humiliated by their parents. It is not uncommon for the father figure to also be quite rough-around-the-edges; he may be part of the group of men who, as children, were mean themselves. In other words, a more aggressive, rude, violent paternal figure makes these boys feel very bad and misunderstood at home too. **Attacked and humiliated mostly by other males, including those who should protect them (fathers, older brothers and other relatives), they grow up feeling angry towards men.**

fifteen

Boys who are pretty, chubby, less aggressive, more fearful, unaccustomed to competitive sports, interested in cultural and artistic pursuits, and whose father figures are violent and demand a virility that is confused with crudeness, reach puberty in a very delicate state. They have, obviously, been influenced by what has happened to them and feel deeply insecure and unsure about their ability to lead a sexual life like the one expected of them. It isn't easy to forget the times they were humiliated, the physical and verbal aggression, in which they were called names that indicated that it was "obvious" they were already gay. They reach puberty doubting their sexuality. Things couldn't be any different.

Most reach puberty angry at men and afraid of approaching women. They fear they won't live up to expectations or be sexually competent. The presence of fear makes it very hard for them to feel visual desire for women, so characteristic of masculinity. On the other hand, very good-looking ones realize that they are the object of visual desire of other men who are further down the path of homosexuality. Vanity thrives on this kind of gaze. As such, many good-looking boys come to enjoy being the object of desire, a satisfying feeling more commonly experienced by women.

At the same time, they don't feel desired by women, at least not in the same way as they do by men.. Afraid they will fail when they get intimate with women and realizing that they are desired by some men, they will probably have their first experiences with the latter. They are satisfying, because sexual pleasure doesn't depend on the type of partner and can even be obtained on one's own. Their enjoyment of this kind of contact reinforces the idea that they are, in fact, homosexual, a conclusion I believe to be mistaken.

Another very relevant factor reaffirms that they are homosexual in their minds: the fact that penetration gives them great pleasure. Parents fear that their sons will choose homosexuality, but in fact, anal penetration is actually very pleasurable for most men. **The stimulation of the prostate gland causes arousal and can even provoke ejaculation without the penis being touched. When this happens, it is as if the young man's "vocation" for homosexuality has been confirmed; he feels an inexorable, definitive member of the group.**

This is yet another example of flawed thinking derived from the lack of honest information transmitted by society about sexuality. The truth is that countless heterosexual men ask their partners to penetrate them with all manner of erotic instruments. They always feel very ashamed about it and often suspect they are not actually as manly as their female partners would like. **Men have always found sodomy pleasurable and it does not imply, under any circumstance, a vocation for homosexuality. The only thing it implies is that it is a pleasurable act that is also prohibited in our sexist culture, which sees it as an open door for two men to feel a "wrong"[14] kind of sexual pleasure.**

We cannot forget the anger that these boys feel towards other boys (and men in general), because of the way they were treated in childhood and early puberty. The consistency and regularity of the awful way they were treated doesn't let them forget – or forgive – what was done to them. Many were verbally attacked and humiliated; others suffered physical aggression. They didn't react because they didn´t think they had the necessary aggression in them. They didn't do it for fear they would come out worse off in the case of retaliation. Many are unable to be physically aggressive because they don't recognise themselves easily in the role of aggressors, held back by pity or guilt; in other words, it isn't always because they are afraid of getting beaten up, since they are already the ones who get beaten up more often. **They didn't react and didn't forgive. They carry around enormous hurt and anger, all directed at men, especially the most manly ones.**

[14] If we had to define homosexuality, like heterosexuality, it would be related to the sex of one's partner, and not sexual practice itself.

Flávio Gikovate

These same boys tend to get along well with girls. This also doesn't help much in this phase, as they seem to have more girlish behaviour than they should. They don't feel hurt by girls or bear them any resentment. With girls they establish friendships, exchange confidences and intimate secrets. They act freely and spontaneously, in a manner they can't around other boys. In a world polarized between two genders, they see themselves as acting and thinking more like girls. This kind of behaviour can reinforce the hostility directed at them by most other boys, who discriminate against them even more. Their childhood anger grows with these new aggressions.

From the outset of my ruminations on sexuality, I have always stated my conviction that this instinct is naturally related to aggression. I believe this to be true of the entire animal kingdom, including ourselves. It may have served the mechanisms that evolutionists consider so important, since the most powerful males really do fare better in the process of perpetuating their genes. **If sexuality immediately correlates with aggression, rather than friendship and tenderness, and these more sensitive boys are friends with girls and feel angry towards men for having humiliated them so insistently, it isn't much of a leap to suppose that visual desire – which is naturally directed at the female body – intervenes and the male body comes to be the focus of desire.**

I never think about the matter without taking into consideration the range of components that I have tried to dissect. I believe they work concomitantly, with a predominance of one ingredient or another in each case. These factors include: male beauty; repressed anger; identification with the female gender and consequent rebelling against one's biological sex; random, satisfying homosexual experiences during puberty; a lack of desire for female figures, stemming from friendship and companionship – especially in the face of the fear of not being capable of performing the male role satisfactorily. And so on. **The more factors involved, the more solid and stable the behaviour they determine. As I have explained here, the way families react to the "risk" that their sons might be homosexual only increases it.**

Twenty years have passed since I first pointed out the strong correlation, present throughout our culture, between homosexuality and aggressiveness. I made reference to something that has always caught my attention: the use of swear words referring to sexual practices between two men to insinuate and threaten others with the hypothesis of being involved in such situations. These are the harshest things one person can say to another. There would be no reason to use such expressions to such ends unless gay sex really did correspond to something strongly laden with aggression.

Another aggressive characteristic that I see in many men (especially gay men) is a kind of subtle, sharp humour, in which there is an evident nasty streak. It is more common among very intelligent individuals, sometimes very successful among men and women. In my mind, it is an indication of the presence of rancour and resentment, expressed in this manner. Wicked humour is yet another sign of the strong connection between sex and aggression.

Many gay men's biggest sexual fantasy is to be "possessed" by a straight man. When they submit to them, they feel great pleasure at bringing onto their "turf" precisely those who parade as macho-men and treat anyone different to them with disdain and scorn. It is a subtle form of domination and revenge very typical of what also takes place in sadomasochism: when the one who serves gives their partner pleasure, they gain some power over them – the dominated also dominate! The path of these fantasies and practices is that of anger and revenge; they don't contain a drop of positive feelings, and at times some kind of financial reward received by the heterosexual is a part of the process – which can be understood as an advantage or imply great humiliation.

Another striking aspect of the gay male world is that their diversity isn't always well accepted by other gay men. There appear to be prejudices among them: more sensitive, effeminate ones are looked down upon by those whose behaviour is more masculine. There are two types of more masculine ones: the discreet ones, who go out of their way not to show that they are homosexual; and those who adopt the standards of conduct typical of each era; in other words, they have a

Flávio Gikovate

particular hair style, work out and wear tight t-shirts to show off their good physique, or other indicators that allow them to quickly recognise their peers. They want to make it clear that they belong to a special "tribe", just like other groups that like to be seen in a specific manner – Goths, certain kinds of drug users, millionaires who like being recognised as such, intellectuals, etc.

As a rule, these subgroups tend to keep to themselves. More masculine gay men don't have a lot to do with more effeminate ones and don't sexually desire them (on the contrary; as I mentioned previously, they are more likely to be interested in very rough-hewn heterosexual men). Even in cases in which more or less stable emotional ties are established, there are few partnerings of individuals who do not – at least in terms of appearance and conduct – display the same kind of social behaviour. A greater degree of discretion indicates that the person is not particularly interested in shocking others; either because their professional activities demand it of them or because they don't bear much resentment toward other people. Homosexual men with more overt mannerisms use their more extravagant ways to shock and avenge themselves of the people who have given them a hard time their whole lives.

sixteen

It is time we reflected a little on the subject of emotional ties. **Given the more aggressive nature of the appearance of sexual desire between two men, and also because the criteria of fascination and admiration are not always simple, it stands to reason that these men will have enormous difficulty becoming emotionally involved. Many recognise this and don't even try to look for partners in the hope of establishing romantic ties. The majority of homosexual men live alone and spend most of their lives seeking sexual partners with whom they form ephemeral ties of little depth.** I cannot say exactly how many of them are in solid, stable, long-term relationships with same-sex partners, but I think they are a minority.

I have already said that there are problems among heterosexual men too, since the association between sex and aggression encourages people to seek inadequate partners as far as character is concerned. But here the issue strikes me as more evident, as those who are not fully satisfied with their sexuality will find it harder to appreciate partners who are similar to them, which further closes the doors on romantic possibilities.

Sex
Flávio Gikovate

Those who are fine with themselves and their sexual preference do, of course, become romantically involved with their peers, a situation in which they experience the same problems as heterosexual men: they almost always choose partners who are their opposites in terms of temperament and character (more generous types are attracted to more selfish types).

The absence of big commitments regarding the creation of professional and financial alliances, along with the fact that they don't have children, increases the instability of the relationship. In other words, after a series of misunderstandings and fights, the ties are more easily broken. Among the heterosexuals who get married, the formal act of marriage does bring with it a greater dose of perseverance and more intense effort to preserve the relationship. Financial issues and children also make separation much more difficult. **The instability of homosexual pairs is also reinforced by the issue of sexual fidelity: few remain faithful during their years together. They are two individuals with male characteristics, very keyed in to the pleasures of promiscuous sex** – as we shall see further along. Couples don't always behave the same as one another. As such, jealousy is very strong and often plays a part in the severing of ties.

Gay men who stay together for decades have probably accepted the fact that the intensity of their sexual desire for one another cools as time goes past and as they develop a good quality loving relationship and companionship – precisely what tends to happen between heterosexual individuals who really love one another. It is likely that many learn to turn a blind eye to superficial sexual indiscretions that men in general like so much, particularly homosexual men. They do so because they also have this kind of experience.

These considerations take us into extremely complex terrain, in which a number of reliable explanations have yet to be found. I describe the facts more than interpret them, not because that is all I want to do, but because I don't feel I am armed with an arsenal of concepts that allow me to advance very much for now. **The taste of some gay men (and in this aspect lesbians are radically different) for vulgarity, for sexual encounters with random multiple partners in public spaces, such as saunas and clubs, was common in the 1960s and 70s.** These encounters became a lot rarer in the 1980s due to the appearance of Aids. They did not disappear, however, and continue to be an important part of the practice of some and the imagination of many others.

Men have always been fonder of casual and promiscuous sexual practices than women. Women who participate in such activities almost always do so for money. Brothels have always been around, and there men found women available for all manner of sexual activities, including group ones. These women usually inhabited such environments because they had been kicked out of home for losing their virginity before they were married – which was standard until just a few decades ago. Nowadays, many work in the field because they chose to and aim, above all, to improve their financial situation. A few believe that brothels are places where they can meet people who are interesting and socially well-positioned, sometimes even dreaming of the possibility of becoming emotionally involved with them – which occasionally happens. This sometimes takes place with the help of alcohol or other drugs (cocaine in particular) to overcome any emotional difficulties. Many prepare to leave the profession and go about getting professional qualifications in order to do so. Others, more immature, end up getting drawn into drug use and are swept along in its dramatic consequences.

Men have biological characteristics that have always made it easier for them to indulge in casual sexual practices: they are dominated by visual stimuli. Thus, any context in which there are visually stimulating factors (whether homosexual or heterosexual in nature) immediately excites them. Exotic garments that enhance certain body parts, such as leather clothes, are already enough to get them aroused and make them want to get closer to the situation that stimulated them. **Visual stimuli are easily produced and cost little (i.e., they don't necessarily require luxury) and reflect availability and ease of access (i.e., open doors for the quick realization of desire). This is what we commonly refer to as "vulgarity".**

Another biological characteristic that makes this kind of casual encounter easier has to do with the fact that

Flávio Gikovate

men clearly experience the previously mentioned refractory period: after they ejaculate, there is an enormous release of sexual tension, and they feel wound-down, light and sleepy. Women do not feel like this after orgasm, making it difficult for them to take as great an interest in casual sex as men do. Many women (once they are adults, of course) don't even enjoy masturbation, because they often feel more aroused than relaxed afterwards. Those who hope to have the same kind of reaction as men end up disappointed and give it up. Others, because they don't understand, are angered by the male desire to relax and sleep after sex.

In men, desire is quelled in an absolute and extremely satisfactory way. For a certain number of hours (or days), they are free of this intense erotic pressure. Sexual stimuli reawaken their desire, however, such that even those who regret having participated in some kind of "vulgar" or "dirty" activity end up returning to the same places.

If some straight men are fascinated by these places (where hygiene usually leaves something to be desired and the atmosphere seems to disqualify everyone present), what can be said about some gay men? **Straight men must always pay to frequent places where casual sex is easy and immediate, since most women are not interested in this kind of activity, unless it is how they earn their living. Some transvestites also behave like female prostitutes, that is, they have sexual exchanges with the main objective of obtaining money.** In fact, the world of transvestism is surrounded by enormous enigmas that have yet to be deciphered. Their "clients" are generally not gay men, but curious straight men, fascinated by these hybrid men-women. Most straight men who go to transvestites do so with a view to being anally penetrated by them. They may consider it a "lighter" kind of homosexual practice, which gives them a more acceptable way to experiment the undeniable pleasure of anal penetration.

If there wasn't any prejudice attached to the subject, and straight men felt they had the right to anal pleasure in their erotic experiences with their partners, maybe they would be less fascinated by transvestites. **Contrary to what most people think, I believe that the end of prejudices tends to reduce the frequency of the practices they aim to impede. In life in general, and sex in particular, all you have to do is prohibit something and people will want it more!**

It is hard to imagine a context more favourable for promiscuity than a relationship between two men. Both are visually stimulated and because they both experience the refractory period, they are fully satisfied with this kind of practice. Additionally, they are not afraid (as many women are) of "losing" themselves in their desire and being unable to regain their calm and rationality, since the refractory period is guaranteed and the man knows he will regain full control of himself – even if he has used sexually stimulating drugs or medications.

Because they both enjoy themselves equally, there is no need for financial intermediation. In other words, what is at stake is almost always reciprocal satisfaction through crude practices, which are often aggressive and highly vulgar. **There appears to be an enormous fascination with what isn't born of culture, as if the overall objective were to return to the animal kingdom, stripped of any modesty or limits. Some have erotic experiences with countless partners in a single night, entirely indiscriminately. They haven't the slightest interest, in this context, in any kind of intimacy or exchange of ideas, etc. The erotic stimulus seems to be fed, among other things, by an absolute lack of interpersonal meaning.**

This environment, often called an "underworld", is often frequented by some of the world's most sensitive, intelligent and creative individuals. It is often shocking and hard to understand how people so concerned with everything beautiful, of the highest quality and value, can be found having erotic experiences with unknown partners in dirty, smelly public toilets. They almost always do so without taking the necessary precautions to protect their health, and risk contracting serious diseases with complicated prognoses.

What do these people, who dive wholeheartedly into such surprising situations, want to tell us? The only observation I feel I can safely make is that such practices indicate clearly and unequivocally how personal our sexuality is; that is, the partner is irrelevant, since such encounters often take place in the dark corners of nightclubs. **I am also convinced that the online world of ero-**

Flávio Gikovate

tica is capable of substituting this aspect of human sexuality advantageously, making masturbation something acceptable, that doesn't need to be hidden! There will, however, still be a fascination with the aggressive, resentful, rebellious and even somewhat exhibitionist nature of these behaviours, and I think it will be harder to reconstruct these things via the internet.

seventeen

I cannot neglect to briefly discuss female homosexuality. It has its own characteristics and shouldn't be thought of as the female counterpart of what goes on between men. In terms of sexuality, most societies treat boys and girls very differently, just as they do men and women. We need to get used to treating the female psyche as something with intrinsic peculiarities, and there is no better subject than homosexuality in which to try to understand a little better the differences, both biological and cultural, that help make up the identities of men and women.

In the past, our culture was ruled by male interests, many derived from men's enormous envy and fragility in the face of women's sensual power. Women have always awoken strong desire in men at the mere sight of their bodies, which places men in an initial situation of inferiority: they need to approach them and try to be well received by them. This has, obviously, always favoured the most beautiful, attractive women, and it is also easy to understand that less attractive women feel at a disadvantage and highly envious.

What men did in the past is well known: they excluded women from socially valued and well-paid ac-

Flávio Gikovate

tivities. They obtained power through status and money, in order to neutralize women's sensual power. They lauded the advantages of being men and, as a result, boys always felt privileged, superior to girls. Boys' games were treated as more important than girls' games, which imitated traditional women's activities and were seen as less important.

If we think about it objectively, it appears that men managed to convince themselves and women that they are members of the stronger sex – and not just physically, which is their only real area of superiority. Everyone used to think it was best if a couple's first child was a boy (and traces of this prevail to this day), as they would be able to pass down the family name and take over family businesses. **Girls were led to envy the male condition somewhat. It is possible that in some eras penis envy was much more common. When I was young, there were still many who felt that they were in an inferior position by virtue of their sex, but many were already fully aware of their powers and the male weaknesses that give rise to sexist cultural standards.**

Penis envy isn't – and never has been – universal. It is on the wane, and nowadays few girls feel at a disadvantage. Girls' access to boys' childhood activities has contributed to this (curiously, girls have taken an interest in boy's activities, but there are no signs of the opposite taking place). **In other words, the world in which the genders are converging seems to be using a traditional male standard of reference, which is a shame**

and also a sign that everyone, including women, places greater value on the lifestyle and activities that men have created for themselves. We will have to wait and see what will come of this in the decades to come.

In the past some girls may have felt at odds with the characteristics of their gender, something that is always facilitated and aggravated by difficult relationships with mother figures. In other words, those who had discontent, resentful mothers, who were aggressive and hostile towards their daughters and more sensitive with and devoted to their sons, may well have developed anger towards their mothers and been annoyed by their attitudes and behaviour and the things culturally attributed to women. They recognized that they were of the female sex, but refused to be a part of the female gender and did not adopt the attitudes and activities expected of them. **Anger towards one's mother figure can, as we already know, interfere negatively in the development of a person's sexuality, transforming the object of anger into an object of sexual interest.**

These girls grew up and deliberately developed male dress, gesticulatory and speech habits. They went out of their way to act like boys. They were teased and laughed at by boys, which meant they were somewhat isolated – because they were also not accepted by other girls. They tended not to be the pretty ones, who were noticed immediately and positively because of their appearance. The pretty ones, even in cases in which they had every reason to envy the male condition, had an inkling that in the future they would benefit from this aspect of femininity so valued in our culture built according to male tastes.

As a result, girls who assumed traditionally male (and even somewhat sexist) behaviour from childhood (even more so from puberty and adolescence) were considered lesbians in the making. They were called names that denote a total lack of delicacy and femininity. This kind of woman with manly ways is becoming increasingly rare among younger women, those who entered adulthood after the 1970s and have benefited from the strong unisex tendency in contemporary culture.

Men, of course, showed no interest in approaching these girls, nor did the girls want them to. They assumed the active stance typical of boys and made plays for the girls whom they thought would be even minimally receptive. In this manner they often found partners whose own stance was undefined, who accepted being approached by them or by boys. Sexual encounters between two women, like those between two men, are perfectly satisfying, especially given the fact that vaginal penetration isn't an essential part of pleasure for most women (besides which, erotic "toys" that substitute the penis, sometimes advantageously, have been around for decades). Relationships that begin casually and almost playfully can sometimes evolve into something interesting, since the ingredient of hostility – an essential part of the interpersonal nature of sexuality for most men – tends not to be as strong between women, if not inexistent.

Interestingly, the fact is that the manly female figure so typical of traditional lesbianism is less and less common nowadays, as are gay men with a wealth of effeminate mannerisms. It is also interesting to note that there have always been fewer lesbians than gay men. It is curious to see that today, in this freer world in which professional opportunities are increasingly opening up to women, as with many other aspects of life in society, the number of lesbian relationships is on the rise. More and more girls and women are forming stable romantic relationships with one another.

It is important to note that, in the past, only a small number of girls who weren't happy about having been born without a penis actually imitated male behaviour. Most of them just preferred their games and activities. But they still liked being specially dressed up or given pretty clothes and shoes. They didn't like playing house, much less helping their mothers with housework. With the arrival of puberty and adolescence, they realized how good it was to be the object of boys' desire and quickly swung over to a more feminine lifestyle. They started cultivating the exhibitionist characteristics typical of many women, especially those who take pleasure (sometimes with clearly aggressive intentions) in provoking men's desire. They used their erotic talents to humiliate them.

Flávio Gikovate

These highly provocative women rarely cultivate more typical women's behaviours. They loathe domestic activities, are not always the most dedicated wives and mothers, and are often somewhat lazy about studies and preparing for a more independent economic life. They seem to have (fathomless) energy, however, for working on their personal appearance and everything that can increase their sensual power. They are very pleasing to the male eye, but don't tend to be good sexual partners, as they enjoy exhibiting themselves more than exchanging caresses. They tend to have it easy during their youth, when they have beauty on their side. But the passing years do not smile on them and they often become bitter in later life.

The sexual interests of women with penis envy, manifested as I have just described it, are focused essentially on men. As I have said before, sex tends to accompany aggression; additionally, the emotional immaturity of those who don't accept the frustration of being what they are (part of a given gender) almost always means they have little ability to love. They usually aren't even interested in "naive" erotic exchanges with other girls, so common during puberty and adolescence.

Speaking of which, it should be noted that there is infinitely less social prejudice regarding physical intimacy between women than there is towards physical intimacy between men. Men can barely touch one another in many cultures, and in some handshaking is the limit. None of this is, or was, valid for girls and women in

Flávio Gikovate

general: pubescent girls have always walked down the street arm in arm, held hands like couples do, and have never feared, as men have, that their physical intimacy might imply an irremediable homosexual tendency.

Many girls have had "spicier" exchanges with their closest friends, and this was also part of the experiences of puberty and adolescence in past decades. In the last twenty years "hooking up" (kissing and limited physical exchanges between teenage boys and girls who barely know one another, but who belong to the same age group and social class) has substituted many of these more intimate moments between girlfriends. **More recently another interesting, unheralded phenomenon has appeared: more girls are "hooking up" with one another too!** It is new because it is not an exchange of caresses within a context of discretion (or even secrecy) between two girlfriends who know and trust one another. "Hooking up" is always a public practice.

What does this mean? In my opinion, it indicates that we are entering an era in which women are going to make bisexual practices a norm, exactly as they learn in the erotic films they can easily see on cable TV and the internet. They are going to have physical relationships just as naturally with partners of both sexes. Many will, of course, prefer one kind of intimacy over another; however, technically speaking, both will be satisfactory. Often two women will be together with one man, just like in the films. A woman may even have physical encounters with two men, but then the situation is completely different, since most men don't touch one another under any circumstance. **Two women and one man create a completely different kind of intimacy than two men and one woman, precisely because male prejudice towards homosexuality is still very strong.**

But this isn't the most interesting aspect of this tendency, not least because I don't believe that group sex experiences lead to stability or go beyond a desire to satiate the curiosity of those who are becoming adults. The most interesting thing is that the number of girls who prefer to establish emotional and sexual ties with same-sex partners is growing. It is hard to say what comes first: sexual interest or emotional intimacy. **The fact is that good-looking girls, who are not at all masculine in their ways, who in the past would have successfully found boyfriends, are now finding girlfriends.**

Families are surprised, and it is to be expected, as they didn't see it coming. I don't even think the girls themselves knew it was going to happen. They entered into emotional and sexual relationships with same-sex partners due to a series of facilitating circumstances in contemporary life. We still don't know exactly where this tendency will lead, as the processes involving life in society are curious and, at times, pendular.

At any rate, it is always productive to pose hypotheses about current tendencies, because it can help make more accurate predictions and give our ruminations greater verisimilitude. I have already mentioned the first variable: we are looking at a much more permissive social context, in which girls have begun to do openly what they used to do in secret – experimenting with stronger sexual exchanges that can lead to orgasm. In this manner, they realize that they can feel sexual pleasure of great intensity. **The fact that the clitoris is the female sexual organ par excellence – and not the vagina, as so many men insist on thinking – creates excellent conditions for sexual fulfilment.**

Diminishing prejudice has also contributed to more girls heading in this direction. Other factors are also worth a brief mention. One has to do with the fact that we live in an era in which physical perfection is worshipped and men and women feel the need to stay very slim and fit. Many girls will end up believing that they fall short of the minimum standard required according to these new criteria – which are just absurd. **If they think that their chances of finding a romantic partner worthy of their aspirations are small, and if they think that getting together with other girls in the same situation will lead to relationships that are both satisfying and much less demanding physically, they may choose this path. It might appear that it was the easiest choice; however, it can also be understood as an act of rebellion against a superficial, exhibitionist culture that cultivates mediocre values, from which many are excluded.**

Another variable that cannot be discarded has to do with the emotional side of things.. Emotional intimacy between boys and girls is usually established, among other reasons, as the result of a connection between sex and aggression, between opposites: one partner is more tolerant and the other more aggressive and hot-headed. These relationships are tumultuous, difficult and full of fights, jealousy and countless obstacles. **Quite often relationships between two girls are founded on friendship, based above all on affinities, where the emotional exchange is intense and pleasurable. There tends to be less jealousy, as they both know that women are less interested in casual sex than men.** They can, therefore, establish sexually and emotionally satisfying relationships of excellent quality, freeing themselves of the need to compete for a spectacular physical appearance, which opens many doors in today's heterosexual world.

There are, therefore, many reasons and advantages that can lead girls towards homosexuality. It is not surprising that the numbers are growing. If I am correct in my thinking, it is legitimate to suppose that, if heterosexual relations don't grow in emotional quality and people don't stop obsessively worshipping physical perfection (especially women's), the number of lesbians will continue to grow. It is interesting to note that, in this case, the term "homosexual choice" really does apply.

eighteen

I think the complexity sex has acquired in our species is more and more surprising. While in the beginning it was a strong instinctive impulse related to reproduction (and perhaps for this reason associated with the aggressiveness of the men who were better at having their way with women, who weren't always so numerous or willing), it now occupies a tremendous amount of space in the imagination of most, especially younger members of society. The association between sex and aggression still exists and is very present. Maybe one day it can be, if not undone, at least attenuated, which will depend on the paths our culture takes.

Currently, we are facing unequivocal facts: most women are attracted to more aggressive (or even inconvenient) men, just as men are more attracted to women who display themselves more overtly – and are very selective about whom they allow to approach them. **Generically speaking, we can assume that we still bear strong traces of our sex life in primitive times. We like to use terms like "hunt" as a synonym for going out to flirt, which is also equivalent to the act of going into the jungle in search of a female, who nowadays must**

be enticed and seduced with lies rather than by means of physical force. Vigorous insistence, however, remains very welcome among women who, because they feel desired, allow themselves to fall into the same trap many times over the years.

Everything seems to suggest that, sexually speaking, we have evolved less than we think. Our fantasies are essentially "mammalian" and involve breaking with the norms that all cultures have imposed on the full expression of our animal sexuality, without which it would have been hard to establish any kind of stable social order. Restrictive norms are almost always connected to one woman and one man and forbid any other partners. **The imagination becomes the environment where people can exercise desires that overstep the rules, at least in appearance. The solution of transferring the sexual extravagances that pass through our minds to the world of fantasy seems to be successful, as a rule.** The fact that sex is an essentially personal phenomenon allows us to be richly entertained via our imagination and accompanying masturbatory practices.

There is, perhaps, a little bitterness that reality doesn't produce stronger, more intense sensations than imagined ones. We should always remember that the imagination is intensely stocked with imagery by pornographic films and material on the internet – which, at least as regards this subject, can be understood as an intermediate space between reality and imagination. Is this so-called "virtual reality" real or virtual? I shall return to this subject shortly.

Flávio Gikovate

Populating everyone's fantasies (and the practices of some) are the diverse forms of sex that involve more than two people. **The most common fantasies are those involving a third person in sexual encounters with a stable couple. This third person could be of either sex, but most commonly (and less daringly) this person is a woman, preferably a sex professional. It could also be a friend of the couple who is willing to participate in their fantasy.** The third person could also be a man, and in this case will only have sexual contact with the woman (whose partner becomes the observer and becomes aroused as he watches the erotic scene between them) or, much more rarely, also has sex with the man. We know that the prejudice surrounding male homosexuality is much stronger than that surrounding female homosexuality, such that few men feel comfortable in an erotic situation with another man (especially in the company of their female partners).

Situations involving more people can also include another couple, a condition in which the pairs swap partners, all-the-while watched by their partners who consent, participate and control everything that is going on. These encounters can take place in special clubs or between people who have met personally or via the internet. There are also even bigger events, involving several men (almost always under the influence of alcohol) and women (prostitutes) who go to places reserved for "parties" that are free-for-alls, in which – theoretically – anything is possible. These orgies, always rife with drugs, are part of some people's fantasies and have been put into practice over the centuries by the highest social classes. They are the heterosexual equivalent of what goes on in gay saunas and clubs, where money doesn't always come into the equation as a facilitator of sex between people who don't know one another.

My clinical experience has brought me into contact with countless people who have had the opportunity to put their sexual fantasies with more than one partner into practice. I have accompanied some rather dramatic stories, ranging from one member of a stable couple lashing out against such practices (with the partner being dubiously accused of inciting events) to people meeting more interesting partners and terminating relationships previously considered stable. Group sex with prostitutes tends to quickly become uninteresting, as well as only happening in situations in which the people are not in their normal state of mind. Maybe it is useful in sealing alliances between men, accomplices in acts that need to be treated with discretion, and which may serve other purposes, including things of a commercial nature.

I am not familiar with any stories of group sex experiences that have become routine in people's lives. They appear to leave people somewhat disappointed. The real results are not as interesting as they imagine them to be. There is a practical reason for this, among other things: simultaneous erotic stimuli, contrary to what people may think initially, subtract from one another.

Flávio Gikovate

One plus one equals less than one! Even those who have never had sex with more than one partner at a time know this: if a man performs oral sex on his partner and receives it at the same time, the feeling of pleasure is less than when each act is performed in isolation. And, naturally, the same thing goes for women. The concomitance creates confusion in the nervous system, just as the presence of two strong pains makes us feel each one less. While, in the case of pain, provoking another pain may be beneficial, as far as sex is concerned, fantasies related to simultaneous multiple stimulation are much more exciting than reality.

Many erotic fantasies, when put in practice, are disappointing. It seems that, at least in this phase of our cultural history, they were made to fill our imagination more than to be lived out. This is a curious moment in history, because for the first time we have created the conditions for a freer sex life without it necessarily implying some kind of social disorganization. The individualistic contemporary world depends much less on the stability and solidity of family life, and the fact that people try to live out everything they imagine sexually wouldn't cause any serious practical disorder. Some gay men are proof of this, as they practice sex in a more impersonal manner without it affecting their personal, social or professional lives. Most people, however, are uninterested in concretising such fantasies and are perfectly satisfied with the freedom of their imagination and the virtual world at their disposal.

Sex
Flávio Gikovate

I have given more and more thought to how much our sexuality is being influenced by the world of eroticism and pornography that has come into being through "virtual reality". **Always bearing in mind that sex is a personal phenomenon, this almost interpersonal – but still personal – world is, obviously, a perfect environment for the flourishing of an infinity of situations that are not terribly real, but can be seen or heard through a computer. We can passively watch pornographic films and interviews. We can "interact" with unknown people who are somewhere else with cameras and microphones. We can participate in chat rooms and "meet" people with whom we can arrange real encounters – that may never take place. Men and women generally become aroused enough that, with discrete manipulation, they find their strongest sexual responses, sometimes stronger than with real partners with whom they haven't had any kind of emotional interaction.**

The virtual world is, in my opinion, teaching us a lot about the true nature of our sexuality, especially its personal nature – which includes intense sensations intermediated by the stimulation of fantasising about images or characters with whom we connect for just a few minutes.

It has also taught us a lot about our emotional life, as we often hear stories of people falling in love with people they "met" through the internet. Intimacy is established through written messages that contain sincere revelations about themselves, in which people get to know one another much faster than they do in person.

Flávio Gikovate

It seems that, in the virtual world, the fear of falling in love isn't as intense as it is in the real world. As such, people strike up love affairs – in which they really tend to be in tune with one another – more easily. They aren't always available or willing (brave enough) to take things further, which can bring as much suffering as in real-life cases of rejection. Real-life encounters may or may not confirm what they feel for one another, since new variables come into play that were in the background while the relationship was essentially a fantasy. Here also, a great deal of careful observation and an open mind is required in order to predict the most probable outcome of such experiences.

The virtual world is also sought out by people with more extravagant fantasies. Some men feel enormous pleasure dressing up as women. They want real physical contact with women and look for partners for this kind of experience, which doesn't involve any kind of homosexual fantasy. I don't know how to explain how this kind of desires arises. Others seek partners for their sadomasochistic fantasies, clearly demonstrating the intimate correlations between sex, power and aggression. Many men seek sexual sensations of an anal nature, which both excites them and makes them feel ashamed; and so on. I won't even broach, at least for now, subjects I don't know enough about because I haven't had the opportunity to observe them first-hand, as is the case with paedophilia.

Flávio Gikovate

I would not like to finish these incomplete considerations on such a new subject without mentioning certain problems and disturbing consequences that may arise as a result of the fact that our young people are, more and more, obtaining their sexual education within the virtual world. **Two aspects in particular need to be examined immediately: the first is the fact that people may find real experiences somewhat disappointing, as the things suggested in the world of the imagination are very attractive and stimulating. Whenever reality has to compete with the imagination and the world of ideas, we have the feeling that it is somewhat simple, a lesser copy of the latter. The real world is smaller and not as rich as the world of ideas and thoughts. At least that's how we feel!** When we imagine the many details of a trip, for example, we might imagine wonderful things that don't come to pass when we actually take it. Our young people need to know this so they won't be taken by surprise and find themselves unduly disappointed by real sex. (This could happen with casual sex, which wouldn't be unwelcome!) But from the point of view of romantic ties, they will have to be very well instructed if they are not to become even more confused than the generations before them.

Secondly, the world of pornography may be perpetuating certain myths about sex. I have already discussed and would like to point out the most serious of them once again: vaginal orgasm is not natural for most women. The vagina has a reproductive function

Flávio Gikovate

and is designed to allow the head of a baby – measuring some 15 centimetres in diameter – to pass through it. If it were a highly sensitized zone, the pain of childbirth would be unbearable. Many women may learn to feel enormous pleasure when penetrated by their partners. Some may even reach orgasm in this context. However, it is not compulsory and should not be considered a fundamental part of sex, in spite of what we see in porno films[15]. Men should not go back to thinking, as they used to, that they have to give their partners orgasms through the prolonged – and oft-times tiresome – repetition of acts that have more in common with physical exercise; nor should women demand this kind of response of themselves. If it happens, it should be spontaneously.

What are the repercussions of this myth? It leads women – who don't want to feel incompetent or at a disadvantage in this area, under any circumstances, nowadays – to fake orgasms, imitating what they see in films. In turn, this can make men – who are completely unable to tell the difference between real and fake orgasms – feel rather heroic. It is, in a way, a game that involves a few more ingredients, as we will see in the next chapter.

---

[15] On the topic, there also appears to be a renewal of male concern with penis size, as these films often use "well-endowed" men. While this may be convenient from the point of view of the films themselves, in reality, most women complain that it hurts to be penetrated by a penis much longer than their vagina.

nineteen

We can't discuss sexuality without revisiting the power relations between men and women from time to time, as well as their dissemination in life in society as a whole. **Women's sensual power depends on the existence of an intense visual desire on the part of men, which is experienced as a command. It is curious to think this way about a simple desire, something which, if not realized, merely leaves one with the bitter taste of any frustration. However, perhaps because in primitive times men didn't have to experience this kind of deprivation (using brute force, they could have whatever woman they wanted), and also because refusals bring the peculiar pain of humiliation (a serious affront to their vanity), men have not had an easy time learning to absorb this kind of psychological discomfort.**

We should not forget that women have always been able to refuse the sexual overtures of any man except their husbands (or, in remote times, their husband-equivalent). It has only been in the last few decades that they earned the right to say no, even to their actual partners; previously, they had to fulfil their "marital duties", treated as such because it never passed through anyone's

Flávio Gikovate

mind that sex had to be pleasurable for them too. If we consider that marriages in the past were not founded on feelings of love or voluntary choice, it is probable that men's erotic interest in other women was perhaps even greater than it is today. Prohibitions of a religious nature and even the risk of earthy punishment have never stopped human beings from breakings rules. On the contrary, prohibition only seems to increase desire.

The most beautiful women used to be coveted by many men besides their husbands, and they could take their pick, if they so wished. The men depended on the women's consent for an encounter to take place, which was an unusual situation. It gave rise to a dispute among men to become attractive and interesting in women's eyes, a novelty which may have something do to with the quick rise in productivity and competitiveness in the most sophisticated societies.[16] As was to be expected, this new situation privileged the most beautiful and attractive women. It may also be responsible for the competition between women who seek prominence and power within the community through relationships parallel to marriage.

Competition between men has always been more obvious and direct. Maybe they are more aggressive and competitive due to their hormonal make-up, as it was

---

[16] I don't know how to assess how much this has affected economic life and production processes. But I think it is important to take it into consideration, along with other variables related to the intellectual restlessness that makes us continuously seek progress and practical knowledge – which goes hand in hand with the greed and vanity that so influence us in our quest for prominence.

Flávio Gikovate

an evolutionary imperative for passing on their genes in times past. As such, they set out in search of whatever could open the doors for them to approach the women they were interested in. **They became powerful not only for personal pleasure and victory over their competition, but also because it implied a very special prize: women's admiration. Obviously, for this to work, they also had to deny women direct access to the success they so admired, such that public power was held only by men, who used it to neutralize the sensual power that was women's greatest weapon.**

Powerful men came to have access to the most coveted women. Nothing very different to what can still be seen in certain luxurious, extravagant environments nowadays. **In these circles, power games are out in the open: powerful millionaires parade around with beautiful, provocative women who are almost always much younger than them. They are envied by many, who dream of what appears to be such a dazzling, glamorous life for themselves.** Fortunately, a large portion of the population, especially women, don't see things in this way any more. They seek independence and don't want a partner on whom they will depend and who – sooner or later – will trade them in for someone younger and more beautiful. They don't want to be at the mercy of an unstable situation that, deep down, will be felt as somewhat humiliating and degrading.

Young women today, even the most attractive ones, want to learn, study and prepare for a life that is also devoted to work and building a worthwhile, consistent personal story that is not dependent on their boyfriends' or husbands' whims. Even when they are economically dependent on them, they are not and don't want to be treated by their partners as figures to be exhibited socially, as trophies. They aim for the condition of partner, of an individual with a well defined, permanent role in the family life they intend to help build.

Men are increasingly aware that times have changed, and many younger ones have even lost the motivation to fully devote themselves to intellectual and professional pursuits. It is a shame, but it appears that, for young men, the greatest motivational force used to be seeking some kind of social recognition, which would facilitate access to the women they desired. Until not long ago, 15-year-old boys knew that girls of the same age didn't even look at them. They were focused on boys of 17 or 18, who were already further along in their studies or doing well in some kind of social activity or sport. They preferred older boys because they admired them and imagined they could meet their matrimonial objectives more quickly with them. Everything is very different nowadays, because from around the age of 13, girls hook up with boys of the same age and, it seems, they no longer see men as providers, who can support them in the future. They think this is something they should achieve for themselves. The change has been fast and radical.

Flávio Gikovate

I hope these transformations bring an end to disputes and power games between the sexes. This isn't what we see in the reality of older members of society, however. While striving to attain financial independence, women continue to do themselves up in order to arouse the desire and interest of men. Officially, they do so to hook a stable romantic partner. However, they often take enormous pleasure in showing off and catching the eye of countless men, who try to approach them, almost always without success. In spite of their efforts to become more independent, they continue to admire men who are more successful than themselves, whom they fight over and consider ideal husbands. **There are still relatively few women who consider sensitivity and character virtues the most important ingredients in future intimate partners. They continue to compete for the most successful men, although less intensely than before.**

Many men still see women merely as objects to be hunted and seduced. They feel anger towards them precisely because they desire them and have to run the risk of rejection. They sophisticate their weapons, sharpen their claws and go to battle, trying, in every way possible, to fulfil their objective of getting them into bed, the only situation in which they feel like winners. Women, whose vanity is inflated by the man's insistence, end up giving in and trick themselves into thinking that what they heard contained a scrap of truth. **After the sexual act, the situation is inverted: the man, stripped of his**

desire, goes back to being in control; the woman, for having accepted the intimacy, feels degraded and humiliated. She waits for a phone call the next day as if it will restore her dignity, and – of course – it doesn't come. The man is avenged via this tardy form of humiliation.

What is most curious is that this story may repeat itself countless times. What can one expect of this kind of encounter besides the same ending? What is to be gained in this kind of intimacy, essentially based on a dispute for a fleeting power? How much time, energy and money are spent on doing up one's body with the objective of participating in such a repetitive plot! A society whose economy is based on consumerism (involving mostly superfluous ingredients) has no choice but to stimulate this kind of conduct, in which rancour and resentment can only grow. Human vanity – erotic pleasure derived from attaining prominence and getting people's attention, must delight in it all. It is an instinctive impulse that is hard to keep under control. However, if allowed to go unchecked, it produces absurdities such as this.

I am eternally shocked when I think that men and women with few skills for this evil, aggressive game of lies enjoy being a part of this group. Its members are valued socially, seen as the most sociable, extroverted and (apparently) successful with the opposite sex. I say "apparently", because they generally manage to pick someone up and don't go home alone. They have sexual relations that can't be anything but mediocre (sexual intimacy between two people who barely know one another is rarely more than that) and then find themselves with the problem of having to rid themselves of the other person. How can anyone still consider this a valid form of entertainment, capable of provoking envy in men who don't know how to lie and women who don't know how to seduce with extravagant clothes and provocative gestures and looks?

This is what is called sexual freedom. I don't deny that unexpected sexual opportunities with no ties sometimes have their charm, especially when they take place in a casual manner, without expectations, based on some kind of empathy and identification. If the possibility of continuity arises, such encounters can provide conditions in which two people can get to know one another – and themselves – a little better. **True intimacy is of great help in getting to know oneself. Quality encounters, even if only casual, do happen from time to time. But making casual encounters a lifestyle choice can become tedious and boring.**

It is curious to note that, the minute women agree to go to bed with someone, they seem to feel they have totally relinquished their power. **This is particularly true when they are the type that surrenders to orgasmic pleasures. This is when their behaviour takes on contours of submission incredibly similar to what was typical of women in the past. They feel as if they now "belong" to the man, who loses interest.** As such, from

Flávio Gikovate

a woman's perspective, casual sex should only be engaged in by those capable of "merely" seeking physical pleasure, free of the complex of emotions and feelings that defines the symbolic nature of sex – which most of us carry to this day.

They may have the best intentions, especially those that people the female imagination, always looking for a stable romantic partner. But there is no denying that women make the same mistakes over and over when, stimulated by the contemporary world, they do themselves up and frequent places in which success means being coveted by as many men as possible, bewitched by the desire they provoke in them. They awaken desire, envy and anger. The result is almost always predictable and disastrous. This is not how one finds emotional intimacy. **Eroticism has its own peculiar workings and, in spite of what some would have us believe, has nothing to do with love and friendship. It is not through the quest for physical perfection (hours and hours a week at gyms, surgical interventions, radical dietary restrictions, etc.) that they will be successful in love. This path, increasingly followed by men as well as women, culminates in a kind of eroticism that is biologically and culturally connected to aggression, with all manner of power games and envious hostility.**

The strategy of our socioeconomic world, based on unchecked consumerism, is intimately related to the designs of vanity and people's desire for success in this erotic game of seduce-and-conquer that doesn't lead to any kind of subjective exchange, much less true emotional ties. **Encouraging this kind of eroticism is, thus, in full agreement with the most conservative aspects of our society. The reign of desire, stimulated to a degree by several influential psychological doctrines over the last few decades, can only lead to the worshipping of youth, beauty, wealth and unchecked competition for success.**

Human happiness is not a part of the design; to the contrary: frustrated people adhere more easily to the norms and values of their world. I shall thus repeat what I have written on many occasions: reason – the part of our subjectivity that collects information derived from our emotions and tries to harmonize it with what we observe, all the while respecting our inner values – has been almost inactive. We are assailed by extremely strong cultural pressures that directly set off our instinctive impulses, such that we barely decide anything about life. Instead of being biopsychosocial, we have been biosocial beings. Maximum individual freedom is preached, but we have never been more enslaved and standardised than we are now.

20
twenty

What can we expect from here on? More of the same, increasingly leading people towards consumerism, competition, envy and rivalry? Or can we expect some kind of reversal of the process, like a pendulum that goes as far as it can in one direction, then swings back in the opposite direction? I have kept a fairly optimistic outlook on the subjects I study, always hoping for positive changes in a relatively short period of time. And I have been systematically wrong.

Good ideas are not enough to change the direction of a community, but change is possible within the lives of individuals and families. In this area, I am as hopeful as always, as I have witnessed important changes in many good-willed individuals seeking happier, more satisfying lifestyles. However, I need to be more realistic as regards collective change, knowing that any small transformation should be considered very welcome. Moreover, we need to accept that ideas can interfere positively, but don't have the same powerful influence as changes in society resulting from technological advances – also derived from ideas, but more geared towards practical life. They are produced by restless minds, which are often exploited by entrepreneurs who are hungry for power and money above all.

I have repeatedly insisted that the biggest, most relevant technological innovation, as far as sexuality is concerned, is the growing importance of what we call virtual reality, an interesting term because it indicates that it is, in a sense, a new kind of reality that is processed in a new dimension. **Sex, an essentially personal phenomenon that has always fed, more than anything, on what is produced in our imagination, seems to work wonderfully with this new world created by information technology.** The porn industry has received an extraordinary boost in the last few decades. Relationship sites are visited by people of all walks of life; sites more directly focused on all kinds of sexual activities – orthodox and heterodox – also have an increasing number of visitors, such that all manner of fantasies and desires find outlets.

Given the characteristics of our sexuality – which requires certain kinds of visual stimuli or fantasies to arouse us so we can stimulate our erogenous zones and derive pleasure from it – participation in the virtual world is likely to gain more and more space in people's lives. This will be particularly true for those who are not in stable, good-quality relationships – that is, most of the population. It may even be the case with those who are satisfied with their real relationships. Most people are highly curious about sexual matters, growing up, as they do, in a world in which different forms of repression make them want to cross the line between what is forbidden and what isn't.

The variety and ease of this new "virtual-real" world with such a vocation for eroticism may come to compete with (and even have an advantage over) casual sex, so enjoyed by men and attempted by women who want to feel freer and more independent. Reality, evidently, contains some ingredients that set it apart from the virtual world. I think the most significant are preparations for the "hunt": women set about buying attractive clothes, doing themselves up in order to be more interesting to men, splash on perfume, practice smiles and gestures in front of the mirror, and so on. This ritual already contains erotic elements connected to vanity, a pleasure associated with the signs of desire that they will most likely receive hours later in a bar or nightclub. Men's preparation is more discreet and, in spite of all of the industry's efforts to make them equally as concerned with their physical appearance, the main repercussion appears to be men's greater efforts to work out in order to stay in shape and maintain their ideal weight – which has become a truly universal concern.

Those who are good at the game of seduction may continue to enjoy their nights out, almost always fuelled by lots of alcohol or other narcotics. It may be that their bodies hold up well and the unpleasant after-effects don't affect them too much. Maybe it doesn't bother them to go to bed with women they hardly know, whose

Flávio Gikovate

sexual tastes and preferences they don't know (which is reciprocal). Maybe the feeling of victory (on both parts) for having managed to seduce someone new makes up for all the discomforts that I have already described.

But what to say about those who are not so successful in such endeavours and return home alone? One can imagine their frustration. Shier, less aggressive men don't approach women who interest them unless the women send them unmistakable signals that they will be well received. Less daring women, who aren't as attractive or who are a little overweight are afraid of showing signs of acceptance because it may lead to nothing, making them feel extremely humiliated. Nothing happens for either party. And even if there is an approach, they aren't always good at making small talk or saying the bold things that one must on such occasions. It isn't fun for them; rather it brings great suffering. These are nights of frustration and pain. They subject themselves to this discomfort because the cultural norm requires single people to go out in search of company and because staying home on a Saturday night is depressing. **They follow the norm and are forced to recognise that they don't have the social skills that are expected of them. They come out the losers.**

I don't think it is absurd to imagine that most people, especially introverts and those who appreciate more meaningful conversation, begin to prefer and participate more actively in events in the new world of the internet. There, things are easier for them: their initial conversations are in writing and there is time to think about their answers. Also, it isn't hard to get rid of someone who proves to be uninteresting or whose ignorance quickly becomes evident through the way they write. Physical appearance is still considered important, but on a much smaller scale. People can get to know one another a little better and "talk" more than in a nightclub, where the music hinders any kind of communication beyond exchanging looks.

Intimacy may – or may not – develop a little more before they think about sharing their erotic fantasies. They may "meet again" another day. They can abbreviate the discomfort related to what happens after climax. They don't run the risk of running into people whose smell they don't like, or contracting a sexually transmittable disease, or spending money for nothing. They don't have to get drunk and feel ill the next day, and can spare themselves the bother of hooking up with partners who don't know how to satisfy them sexually and with whom they can't express themselves openly because they don't know them well enough.

Sexual activities on the internet are a new source of wealth and involve important economic interests. However, they are damaging to many sectors of the economy that produce material goods: the clothing, cosmetic and perfume industries, among others, will be harmed if the number of people who prefer the virtual world grows. A minority of people are successful in their efforts, via material acquisitions, to attract the attention of the opposite sex. Most men and women end up following patterns of consumption due to the beliefs and pressures of the world around them, not because they feel truly rewarded for their expenditure.

I think the biggest obstacle to be overcome in order for "virtual reality" to gain more ground and surpass more contrived "real" encounters (the kind that take place at certain times and places frequented by singles) in importance and interest is the belief that masturbation is a less honourable, poorer form of sexual pleasure than real encounters. That is, we place more value on the act of touching and being touched by someone else than the act, repeated since the tenderest age, of stimulating our own erogenous zones. **A man may go to a brothel and meet a woman whose name he doesn't know, who addresses him generically as "love"; pay for sex (often performed with lagging enthusiasm and a good dose of falsity); and still leave thinking it was worth it.** He will probably consider it much more interesting than watching a porno film, becoming aroused and masturbating, resulting in the delicious feeling of relaxation and sleepiness that he has known since adolescence – when he became initiated in this practice.

I can't help but think that masturbation is much more interesting and satisfying than a man having sex with a prostitute or a woman having sex with a fumbling man who has no real idea what she needs to have an orgasm – and which doesn't even provide her with the relaxation that it affords men anyway. **In the virtual world there are no caresses, which must be practiced individually as in masturbation. Apart from this, all the rest is possible, with greater freedom and intimacy even. People aren't as afraid of exposing themselves, and can visit "places" they wouldn't dare to in reality, such that they may even broaden the frontiers of what they thought was allowed or acceptable in this world of sexual fantasies that really shouldn't be regulated.**

I have little doubt that virtual reality will come to compete on a large scale with casual sex and brothels. I think its importance is still underestimated because it appears, more than anything, to be an activity enjoyed by teenage boys, who are the precursors of this kind of preference. But one day they will be adults, and this world of interests may become stable for them. Girls who are shier, more sensitive and less successful in the "real" game of seduction will probably adhere more quickly to this kind of practice than those who fare better in real situations. Singles and people with more refined tastes will probably seek partners in this arena. There will be many mistakes, with a lot of lying and false advertising going on. But it isn't anything new and is just as common in real life.

Let's rewind a little and consider intimate encounters of a temporary, fortuitous nature. They should not be confused with the casual sex that I have described. They are encounters that happen only a few times in most people's lives. They take place on business trips, holidays and in other situations in which no kind of event of this sort was on the cards. Two people strike up a conversation, discover a good number of common interests and tastes, develop intimacy in a short period of time, are attracted to one another and may have a short fling – perhaps even only a day long.

These encounters are rich and leave a strong impression and satisfying memories. They are situations in which both people know beforehand that the end is nigh, which perhaps even makes them let themselves go emotionally and sexually. When people are mature and lucid enough to understand that continuity isn't possible, even if they come to wish it was, because their real lives are incompatible (they live in different countries, have prior commitments, do not wish to establish stable ties because their professions make it difficult, etc.), **they may still experience intense pain when they part. However, they will be strong enough to overcome the pain quickly and will know how to take extremely valuable lessons from these encounters. They cannot and should not be confused with the casual sex that I have described. They are not encounters that can be actively sought; they just happen – including in the virtual world.**

21

twenty one

I must insist once again, now explicitly in the context of sex, on the need to abandon elitist ways of thinking and seek more democratic solutions for the big issues of subjectivity. It is absolutely essential if we wish to build a society of free human beings with a reasonable amount of self-esteem. When we privilege characteristics that are inaccessible to the vast majority of the population, we produce a collective state of mind prone to unhappiness, negative self-image, anger and depression.

Illusions of this nature are generated every minute. When a person of humble origin achieves some kind of professional or financial success, they attribute it to their efforts and the fact that they live in a society in which there is some social mobility. They say things like, "If I was successful, you can be too." It isn't true, of course, and only serves to feed the illusions of the majority, condemned to remaining right where they are. Social mobility is relative and only a few lucky ones manage to overcome certain limitations. They act like lottery winners: they are the living example of that which probably won't happen to the majority of those who play.

Flávio Gikovate

Living on dreams can bring some hope, but it is illusory. It is great for those who like to fantasise and dream more than they like to live. Maybe it doesn't do so much harm, as far as superfluous things go. But only having illusions as opposed to access to the resources essential for health care, personal hygiene and food, for example, is very serious. Even more serious is our society's tendency to look down on what most people have and worship only that which exists in small qualities and which, inevitably, will be distributed unequally.

As regards sexuality, the situation is very similar. We can value physical beauty and sensual exuberance (rare characteristics that privilege less than, say, 3% of the population) or we can value a person's willingness and ability to truly engage with their partner sexually and surrender to the experience (in favourable conditions, whatever those may be, in a context of companionship and trust). **We can idealize people who have sophisticated their powers of seduction (men who are good at lying and coming on strong, and women who are skilled at showing off, leading men up the garden path) or those who are more spontaneous, who act naturally and, on a night out on the town, don't care who is watching them as they dance.**

We can look up to men who are sexually devoted to a single romantic partner (and are happy that way) or those who are always bragging about their latest conquests, who are always in the company of beautiful women with whom they appear to have little intimacy.

Flávio Gikovate

We can look up to women who are happier having a stable sexual partner who meets their emotional needs (with whom they can let their guard down and do away with the traditional strategy of withholding or giving sexually according to other interests), or those who are interested in new material acquisitions, with which they hope to make themselves attractive to as many observers as possible.

Our society values beauty, thinness, exuberant sensuality, the ability to attract multiple partners, women's ability to attract the most coveted men (the rich and famous, not always of the best character), and doesn't care what really happens to people between four walls. In other words, we are taught to be impressed by appearances rather than facts. Little does it matter that the stunning women parading across our TV screens are unable to let their hair down sexually when they are actually with a partner. They devote themselves to what appears to be most important to them: eliciting desire. Enjoying the pleasures of the flesh takes a back seat.

I sometimes get the impression that desire is starting to occupy a space that doesn't belong to it. It seems to define us more than having a brain capable of producing complex thoughts and reflections, some of them regarding the rights of others. All of our sophistication comes undone in the face of the reign of desire. We are led to think that we are divided into those who

desire and those who are desired. The desired are the privileged and those whose desire is unrequited are unlucky; they will have to find ways to improve their situation if they want to be accepted by the objects of their desire. Highly desired women – and men with the requisites to be accepted by them: wealth, fame, and the ability to lie and deceive – are the heroes of this era of the reign of desire.

All anyone thinks about is desire, and I get the impression that no one is interested (not even those who study the human psyche) in changing this. **It would appear that it is good to want things all the time: material goods that make us more attractive and facilitate access to the biggest possible number of partners; to be desired by those who are desired by everyone else; social and professional positions that open doors to a life in which we can find new, more interesting partners, and so on. I wonder how thinkers like the Roman Stoics (Epictetus and Seneca, among others), who also lived in eras in which customs were very extravagant – would look at this world. They believed that a rich man is not one who has everything, but he who desires nothing.**

Without being too extreme, I think the real role of sex – apart from reproduction, of course – resides in the possibility of having a natural, simple source of pleasurable stimuli that can lead to, more in men than in women, a pleasant state of relaxation related to the end of arousal. It is essential that we change our focus from desire to arousal, reducing the importance that has been attributed to the former. Desire always implies something or someone that is desired: and the thing or person that is desired is, in some way or another, in a situation of privilege and superiority.

Desire supposes hierarchy and almost always involves things that are elitist, that is, not available to the majority. People desire objects that can only be obtained if they possess the material means to buy them. They desire certain women and must live up to certain criteria in order to be accepted by them. They desire certain social positions and depend on the approval of other people in order to achieve them, and so on. We should always remember that the most coveted material goods, attractive women and prominent social positions are limited in number and only accessible to a few privileged ones who, by merit or cunning, manage to get close to them.

Desire is composed of arousal, but it also contains an important ingredient of risk: the challenge of being successful or not. Failure obviously implies suffering, just as success can reinforce the intensity of arousal. Desire is part of a game. Arousal is a very simple phenomenon, without winners or losers. In masturbation, for example, we are all winners! Everything happens according to our fantasies and there are no disputes or rejections. The big pleasure, not always sought due to lack of courage or unawareness, is being able to let oneself be carried away by sexual stimuli without rational control, similar to what happens when we ingest too much alcohol and lose control over our thoughts and actions. It is practically impossible to relinquish all control in front of another person, especially if we are with a partner we barely know and whom we don't trust – or whom we wish to impress.

I believe it would be beneficial to surrender to the pleasures of arousal via masturbation stimulated by sexual fantasies, or exchanges with stable partners whom we trust. In these contexts, conditions are favourable for learning to let go and allowing arousal to go almost to the point of losing control (which may be somewhat frightening at first, but contains no real risk of any sort); this is, perhaps, the best sex has to offer us. It is an enormous source of pleasure, similar to what happens with young children – especially girls – who feel great satisfaction when they touch their erogenous zones with the simple, immediate intention of enjoying the feeling of arousal. Why complicate everything with the act of desiring what is almost impossible and experiencing the torment of frustration and low self-esteem?

Why give up a pleasure accessible to us all (of a highly democratic nature) to devote ourselves to practices with an enormous chance of failure? What society is this that teaches us that the most valuable thing is precisely something we will never be able to have? Why should we accept this kind of arbitrariness? Why should

Flávio Gikovate

we seek sexual or emotional partners who are highly valued for dubious, superficial characteristics, such as beauty and success, when we should look for people who have the character virtues and emotional sensitivity that would help us to live more happily? We should always bear in mind that character virtues are democratic properties, although they are not as well distributed as they could be. People who haven't cultivated them can do so without harming those who already have them; there is always room for more good souls.

The fact that people of dubious character are more sexually attractive is due to desire rather than arousal: such people raise doubt, are a constant challenge and play on our vanity and self-esteem, as we're never sure what they are going to do next. They leave us in a permanent state of uncertainty. It is our cultural tradition to think that challenges renew desire, which isn't untrue. A wife who isn't always available for sex tends to elicit her husband's desire more often than one who is always willing, and vice versa; wives tend to be more interested in sex when their husbands are somewhat complacent about it. They are motivated by the challenge, the wounded pride, the wish to overcome the obstacle.

Tradition also dictates that the desire of couples who have been together for a long time fades and that their sex life becomes mediocre and increasingly poor. Maybe it is true in terms of desire, which requires novelty and challenge. But if we consider arousal (and the fact that it comes mostly from tactile, rather than visual, stimuli), we will reach very different conclusions than those suggested by the culture of desire. In reality, erotic exchanges between people who feel comfortable in one another's company bring the same arousal as in the beginning of the relationship. If arousal can be produced individually, through self-manipulation, and be a source of pleasure throughout life, why can't the same thing happen between two people who enjoy one another's company?

Visual desire inevitably wanes with the passing years. Firstly, because it is fuelled, like all desires, by challenge and novelty. Secondly, because age doesn't make bodies more seductive. In fact, in this world governed by desire, growing old has become an enormous nightmare, especially for women – above all, those whose beauty and sensuality attracted a lot of attention when they were young. It stands to reason that those most devoted to cultivating this kind of virtue will also be those who will try hardest to perpetuate their appearance by means of aesthetic surgery. I have no doubt that all of this inevitably leads to frustration, as the most brilliant surgical intervention cannot completely erase the work of the passing decades.

Access to medical resources that can minimize the weight of the years is elitist in nature. Most of the population will never be able to afford such things (nor are they always successful). **I am averse to any kind of elitist intervention designed to reignite desire, which I see**

as an obvious commitment to the worst aspects of ourselves and our society.

I understand that desire and vanity are believed to have contributed greatly to the construction of works that characterise humanity, such as the great discoveries and changes that we made to our primitive, inhospitable habitat, driven by a yearning for prominence and sexual and material advantages. I also know that many of the goods produced have benefited large portions of the population. Epidemiologists have made important discoveries about the life cycles of certain microorganisms that had such a negative impact on our ancestors' quality of life, and the ambition and determination of some have brought advantages for all of us. Maybe without the erotic stimuli of desire and vanity we would have advanced much less. But wouldn't we have got close to where we are by virtue of the intellectual restlessness that torments many of our most brilliant minds? These exceptional gifts are also rare, elitist qualities. Shouldn't they be at the service of all?

How many of the great wonders of the ancient world, such as the Egyptian pyramids and the Coliseum in Rome, have inspired our admiration? But how many millions of workers died during their construction? I don't believe that reinforcing vanity and elitist desires is the only way to live. Maybe it has prevailed over other possibilities because it is the strongest. I believe we urgently need to rethink this tendency that is now leading to the total destruction of the planet at a frightening speed. **It is time to think about subtracting this erotic ingredient from the forces that rule life in society and bring eroticism back to its true, democratic, inoffensive place: that of gratifying sexual experiences that we can either have alone or in physical contact with partners with whom we are not fighting for anything and with whom we merely want to share pleasurable experiences.**

22

twenty two

A few considerations are called for regarding the delicate question of how to bring sex into the domain of good-quality loving relationships. Those familiar with my work know I am not referring to the vast majority of marital relationships. In these, the ingredient of aggression derived from reciprocal envy – an almost inevitable sub-product of big differences in temperament and character, and the friction they cause – gives rise to a significant force of repulsion and ever-imminent break-up. Because this isn't what people really want, the sexual impulse joins forces with other factors that establish physical and sentimental re-approximation, providing positive reinforcement for the renewal of desire. The husband desires his wife, and the wife, who wants to be desired, is aroused by it. This is a condition in which she is open to sexual intimacy. For a long time this kind of dynamic can be efficient and even reinforce the emotional bond which, in itself, is fragile.

Evidently, when the wife is the selfish, demanding partner, the situation may take on somewhat different characteristics, as such women feel an enormous need to incite desire, then leave their partners frustrated. In this case, everything will depend on the generous, tolerant husband's stance. If he is too indulgent, he will end up accepting the restrictions imposed by his wife with undue docility, which will reinforce her behaviour. If he shows signs that he won't tolerate this kind of manipulation and can find unilateral solutions for his sexual satisfaction, he will certainly be helping his companion to let go of this kind of ploy, of which she is also a victim. **I repeat: excessive, undue tolerance is not a virtue, as it reinforces the worst side of the people around us.**

When the wife is the one with the more generous temperament, she is generally quite available for sex and rarely refuses, because she loves her partner (who doesn't always deserve it), and also because she feels constantly threatened that he might be unfaithful. She takes pleasure in giving and devoting herself in all areas, including this one. More selfish men tend to be good sex partners, always concerned with impressing and pleasing their partners – out of vanity more than anything. They almost never feel unmotivated in the presence of an available woman. It does occasionally happen, however, especially in cases in which they do not have strong sexual impulses and are content just feeling attractive to their partners. In these rare cases, the available wife complains of her partner's lack of interest. She tries to go after him to stir up his interest, which has poor results, as the man feels pressured and nothing is worse for his sexual performance than that.

Flávio Gikovate

Perhaps the first point to be stressed here – regarding the difficulties of bringing sex into quality relationships – has to do with tenderness. Tenderness involves physical manifestations of affection, similar in every way to the caresses that lead to sexual arousal; however, psychologically and symbolically speaking, the connotation is totally different. **We know that love, in its adult version, bears important similarities to what happens between mothers and their children in the first few months and years of life. Tenderness is more reminiscent of a mother's touch than caresses of a sexual nature. Although delicious, these caresses are completely lacking in sensual appeal. They are physical manifestations that give us calm, peaceful, cosy feelings. Nothing at all like arousal, which is similar to what we feel when we touch our erogenous zones.**

As such, not only the romantic words used by adult lovers ("love", "cutie-pie" and others that we also use for babies) but also the caresses given in this context give clear signs that we are looking at a totally asexual situation. We weren't warned, much less prepared, for this, and it can come as a big surprise: a man in love imagines that he will find in his loved one a sexual partner capable of making him feel things he has never felt before. After all, within the cultural context we live in, the dominant thinking is that love and sex go hand in hand and are part of the same instinctive impulse. **If love is so intense, we can expect the same from sex. Sweet illusion! As a rule, the person**

in love feels totally inhibited sexually. The romantic poets probably learned this in practice and ended up describing intense love as being "platonic" (asexual) in nature.

In practice, this means that the woman is highly idealized and placed on a pedestal, which, for men, becomes an insurmountable sexual obstacle, as they feel smaller and inferior. **Idealization does the great disservice of blowing up the loved one's supposed virtues to such an extent that we feel small in comparison. While this doesn't imply sexual difficulties for women (to the contrary, even), for men it appears to become unbearable, wounding their pride and giving rise to insecurity and fears that stop them from achieving erection** – and even when they do have one it can inhibit ejaculation.

Even after the initial phase of somewhat undue idealization has been overcome, when each one can see his or her partner's qualities and flaws more clearly, fully exercising one's sexuality may still be difficult. The situation does become much more comfortable, because some of the inhibitions related to the strong urge to impress and be good enough for one's beloved disappear, just as the fear of letting them down by doing something inappropriate also diminishes. **At this point, lovers start to experience a calmer phase, in which they may even feel comfortable enough to talk more openly about what is happening to them sexually. Obviously, especially in the case of younger couples, it doesn't make any sense to be complaisant about sexual diffi-**

Sex
Flávio Gikovate

culties that arise in this context. **Obstacles were made to be studied, assessed, faced and overcome. What appears insurmountable at one point may not be some time later.**

The first thing to consider is that we have been the victims of incorrect information: that love and sex are a part of the same impulse and that one reinforces the other. **I am convinced there really are incompatibilities and difficulties to be overcome in order to bring together these two impulses, one of an integrative nature (love) and the other individual (sex).** In love, especially early on, there is a strong tendency for people to yearn for fusion. **When discussing the subject in one of his dialogues on love, Plato said, "One cannot desire what one already has."** This appears to be the case, at least initially, with romantic fusion: Lovers have no doubt that they belong to one another, that they were made for one another, that one is an extension of the other. How can we desire a part of ourselves? It's hard.

The second thing to consider is the necessary distinction (increasingly fundamental in my opinion) between desire and arousal. Desire depends on exteriority; the loved one is perceived as an autonomous, independent being, a true "other". Desire implies subject and object: the one who desires and the one who is desired; in other words, two individuals rather than an amalgam of two halves that have become one. It has to do with the act of approaching someone else exterior to ourselves and that person's acceptance of us. It takes on interpersonal connotations when associated with aggressiveness (its most natural and, in a sense, biological association) or love (at least in theory). I shall return to this subject shortly.

Arousal, on the other hand, is a clearly personal phenomenon. It depends on the act of touching oneself or exchanging caresses, and is fundamentally tactile. When produced individually, it is generally accompanied by a wide variety of erotic fantasies, when not reinforced by virtual "interactions" – which are becoming increasingly frequent and are also being practiced by a growing number of women. **When we are with a partner, the fantasies can, obviously, be substituted with visual stimuli derived from watching our partner react to what we do: realizing that we are able to make them aroused with passionate kisses and the stimulation of their erogenous zones can provoke an intense sexual reaction in the one providing the stimulation.**

The exchange of caresses can be simultaneous (which, as I mentioned earlier, tends to diminish the intensity of what one feels because of the concomitance of more than one stimulus) or in turns. Kissing one's partner on the lips is, obviously, simultaneous. After this, however, the man may stimulate the women orally or manually and then the woman may reciprocate. **I don't think too much imagination is required in order to take things from an atmosphere of tenderness to arousal. We just need to be aware that the transition**

Flávio Gikovate

must take place, that it is not a spontaneous phenomenon that will necessarily and naturally happen. A passionate kiss is often the vehicle that intermediates the transition.

Once the transition has been made, and the couple is in the terrain of erotic arousal, it may be wise to stay alert so that it doesn't slide back into tenderness, which is always negative in this context and capable of neutralizing the sexual effects of exchanging caresses. At least, that is, until the partners reach climax, when a return to tenderness is welcome and manifests with even greater intensity. **Climax is a moment of radical solitude, when we are totally immersed in our own sensations; we close our eyes and are no longer in the presence of anything or anyone. The loved one reappears after this, and reencountering them brings with it a pleasure that can only be experienced when sex is practiced within an emotional context.**

I hope I have been clear in affirming that, in the manner in which I have just described it, sexuality is totally independent from desire. The couple comes together and decides to have sex. Desire isn't absolutely necessary. Experience also teaches that most couples who love one another neglect sexual practices sparked by arousal precisely because there is no desire. They sometimes say they forget to have sex. Perhaps desire would help them to remember sex, but we have other means of initiating an erotic exchange. The interesting thing is that these couples who say they don't have sex very often never complain about the quality of it when they do. It is curious that quality seems to diminish interest! Or is it because they already feel fulfilled by other pleasures and joys? There is no harm in insisting on the benefits (even for one's health) of a richer, more satisfying sex life. In other words, happy couples' somewhat negligent approach to sex isn't always such a good thing.

While the exchange of caresses capable of bringing about sexual arousal must be set in motion by a rational action, other things are required for desire to manifest. I am still referring, obviously, to couples who truly love one another. Perhaps the most important thing is to create the context of exteriority, in which, for example, the woman ceases to be someone who "belongs to" and enchants her partner, and transforms, for a few minutes or hours, into any woman. **How does this "magic" take place? The vast majority of couples turn to practical resources. Some woman use raunchy lingerie.** They play the part and act in a manner that may be more extravagant and indecent than normal.

Couples often go to places outside of the home, where their children often sleep in the room next door. In motels, revealing clothes, smutty language and porno films create an atmosphere of exteriority, indecency and vulgarity that do wonders for desire and have nothing at all to do with the emotional context of their everyday lives.

Desire – male desire, at least – rarely arises through an association with love. What ends up happening is a

temporary emptying of the romantic content of the relationship, which is replaced with the vulgarity and indecency so in keeping with our species' and culture's brand of eroticism. Maybe it is easier for women to exercise their sexuality in a romantic context, but I think that feeling desired once again for their physical attributes is also a return to a kind of pleasure that is highly satisfying. In my mind, such moments are very rich and interesting. Love is suspended so that more mammalian manifestations can come through. However, I still believe that love and its peculiarities can provide the richest, most interesting ramifications for personal happiness and the well-being of life in society.

Eroticism, especially in the terrain of desire, seems more related to our ancestral experiences, prior to civilization. It is good to understand this and give it some space to express itself. On the other hand, it doesn't make any sense to think that it is a refined manifestation of our species, much less imagine that freeing ourselves of these impulses governed by desire will lead us somewhere very different to where we are now: a slightly more subtle, sophisticated version of what used to happen in primitive times.

twenty three

My considerations thus far have led us naturally to the epilogue and my final ruminations. I will try to answer two central questions about our sexuality. Firstly, what is its actual role in our subjectivity, what is its weight and importance compared to love? And secondly, what is a truly free person, sexually speaking?

The liberating experiment of the 1960s was founded on the thesis that, if we were able to undo the repressive regimes that society had always imposed on sex, people, especially younger generations, would let their guard down and become less competitive, more cooperative and lead creative lives. This illusory idea was born of the erroneous belief that sex and love were parts of the same instinctive process related to everything vital. **In reality, as I have repeated ad infinitum, sexual liberation ended up being women's open exhibitionism, which sparked more competition among men and rivalry among women than ever before. The youths who wanted "peace and love" went to war and armed themselves to the teeth so as to adapt to an increasingly competitive, exclusive world.**

Technological advances heightened tension between people, as the desire to possess these new goods (especially related to the electronic and virtual worlds) and the yearning for prominence of an elitist nature (whose objective is, among other things, to open the doors to success with the opposite sex) have made friendships increasingly rare. As such, romantic, marital and family relationships are more and more fluid and tenuous.

The rapid ascension of women in the job market, the result of their academic efforts, is another new factor and upsets interpersonal relationships in general. Men are more fragile, and the younger ones are delving deeper into the virtual world, where they don't have to prove themselves in order to be successful with the opposite gender. They are growing more complacent, while girls, who are increasingly aware that they will have to provide for themselves, are proactive. It is still hard to say where this will take us.

A fact worth noting once again is that the quality of sexual relations hasn't improved. Even today, men appear to be unaware that women's greatest sexual pleasure is clitoral. Because most sexual relations take place in an atmosphere in which intimacy has barely begun (if, indeed, it goes anywhere), most women do not feel comfortable explaining what they do and don't like to their partners. Men continue to insist on extracting vaginal orgasmic pleasure from women they hardly know. Not that women don't derive any satisfaction from penetration, but it is symbolic in nature and depends on intimacy, trust and genuine satisfaction at allowing a particular man to penetrate them. And this only comes after weeks of knowing one another.

The emphasis on sex and the idea that the most important thing is to have lots of experiences with different partners runs parallel to an extreme preoccupation with physical appearance, as regards both the body itself and consumerism in general. We know that quality loving relationships between people who have more affinities than differences (especially as regards character) run into countless intrapsychological obstacles: the fear of losing one's individuality; the fear of facing a painful break-up; our fear of happiness, as if it were capable of attracting immense misfortune and suffering. In addition to these problems there is also the fact that, increasingly, sexual desire is more easily directed at less trustworthy people, of dubious character.

If we consider the relationship between sex and desire (that is, the impulse to try to get close to someone in order to establish some kind of sexual intimacy), people tend to be fascinated by the most sought-after individuals, who they try to win over as a kind of victory over other competitors. Additionally, as I have also said before and would like to emphasise, the act of desiring implies hierarchy, such that the desired one holds a power that can only be diffused when they have been won over. This is frequently followed by a series of retaliations on the part of the successful wooer – the one who desired the other originally and felt like the underdog, and now discovers they have the upper hand. There is an atmosphere of war between the sexes (or between two people of the same sex), rather than peace. Much less love.

In quality relationships in which both partners are ready (that is, not so afraid to establish intense ties and commitments), the enchantment comes precisely from discovering great affinities. The more people talk, the more they become smitten with one another. The erotic element takes a back seat and intimacy is built along the same paths as in friendships. **The partners in a loving relationship of this kind are also the best of friends. We know that desire doesn't go hand in hand with this kind of undertaking, as there are no challenges and no one needs to be wooed. People enjoy the intimacy and put up no resistance. The couple develops an atmosphere of tenderness, much like that between a mother and child – which can even hinder, at least in the beginning, the possibility of an exchange of caresses that can lead to sexual arousal. Arousal doesn't depend on desire, which is only present in the context of challenges. But it does require the atmosphere of tenderness to be shed, which – with a proper understanding of the processes involved in romantic love – is relatively easily to achieve.**

It is evident that sex can have more than one role in life. If we are competitive and combative in nature, we

Flávio Gikovate

will live in the reign of desire. We will seek partners who are hard to win over and delight in our glories in this area, as well as in all of the others directly or indirectly related to it – in other words, almost everything that governs our social experiences of an elitist nature. If we are successful, we may bask in our achievements, or feel good that we have incited the envy of our competitors, or be applauded and treated like winners in the game of life. And we are winners in the game of life according to the current code, which doesn't mean that it is the only way to live or that it has anything to with what we might call happiness.

I am not certain that life needs to be understood as a game. I know all too well that it is in this context that people are at their most productive, a condition necessary for a society to be so successful that it out-performs its competitors. I also believe that, especially in the past, less enterprising groups that weren't as good at shoring up their forces were decimated by stronger ones. **I know that competitive capitalism is more productive than a society based on cooperation and sharing more or less equally the benefits of that which they manage to produce. But I also know that if we don't change tack in the way we live, both individually and collectively, we will be charging headlong toward the abyss of low self-esteem and depression in most of the population, and an irreversibly imbalanced planet.**

Isn't it time we revisited the way we think about sexuality and tried to see it in a different light? That is, can we

Flávio Gikovate

not put an end to the reign of desire and think more about arousal? In practice, this has several ramifications. The first and most important is that this way of understanding sex has, above all, more to do with the extraction of intense, satisfying sensorial pleasure which this impulse can provide, starting in our second year of life. **We can abandon the world of sex as competition and conquest and make it a source of fun and pleasure, something we can enjoy and which can be done – at least individually – wherever one wishes without any kind of exceptional effort. Arousal is democratic – a pleasure available to everyone. Desire, on the other hand, is elitist, as it is only enjoyed by the winners – and humiliates the vast majority. The exploration and discovery of all the paths and nuances of eroticism that can be set in motion in the body brings great satisfaction in life.**

So why not establish good-quality loving relationships with like-minded partners and enjoy the erotic exchanges that provoke direct, tactile arousal and the wonderful feeling that we are giving our loved ones pleasure? With them, we will have the intimacy to share sexual fantasies of any kind and feel comfortable enough to teach them the parts of our bodies that most arouse us. With them, we can explore the delights of intense eroticism – which, beyond a certain intensity, is solitary in nature, as we become absorbed in sensations. We then reappear to our loved one, which brings with it a wonderful feeling of reunion.

Sex
Flávio Gikovate

In the context of love and arousal, sex plays a secondary role. In the domain of desire, it is the protagonist. We must each decide how to position ourselves. I have no doubt that a loving relationship in which sexuality plays a supporting role is a more harmonious, gratifying and essentially democratic way to live. I also think that this is the path to a less competitive social order, which will aid the survival of our species, threatened by its own greed.

I know that these considerations may seem somewhat conservative, since they are similar in some ways to traditional religious thinking. Love as an element of salvation is part of many discourses of this nature. Personally, I am not bothered by this. On the contrary, I have always thought that those who went before us managed to amass an important body of wisdom and had more calm and time than we do for deep reflection on certain issues. Obviously, my views are adapted to a new reality and the way I see love isn't exactly the same, just as my praise of sexual arousal as an essential part of the pleasures of a loving couple doesn't have much to do with the idea of sex for reproductive purposes only.

I don't believe that men who think they can't miss an opportunity to approach a woman are sexually free. This kind of person, perhaps still the majority in certain cultures (such as Latin ones), isn't slave to his desire, but to his duties as a "macho man". **He adheres to the "real men never miss a chance to copulate" tradition.**

Flávio Gikovate

The situation is worse than in primitive times, when men were "allowed" to approach whichever women they desired. Now they "have to" approach them. This "stud" cannot fail either; that is, his sexual performance must be in accordance with what he expects of himself (as well as the current standard). As such, he will have to maintain an erection for a certain number of minutes, have sex and, if possible, give the woman an orgasm (not only because it pleases him and to feed his vanity, but also because it is his manly duty), **ejaculate with a certain intensity, and so on.**

Today's standard of excellence is taken from porno films, such that many men seek treatment (if they indeed exist and work) to increase penis size and take drugs to maintain stronger erections merely for "recreational" ends, which, in reality, serves two purposes: to impress women and to make themselves feel that they are living up to what is considered ideal. None of this has anything to do with freedom. It is a series of commandments that must be obeyed, as if it were a test that everyone must pass.

While these demands have always tormented the male mind, many of them have also entered the female mind. Nowadays, women also need to give a performance similar to that of porn stars: emit noisy sounds that indicate pleasure during insistent vaginal penetration, as well as in anal sex (which, until not long ago, was abominated); practice vigorous and deep oral sex; enjoy having men ejaculate in their mouths and other

practices that didn't used to be on the cards. Previously, they were exempt from all demands, as highly valued women were chaste, showing little interest in sex, but not refusing their "marital duties". The demands have now caught up with them too, and they are no longer free to express what they really feel either. **They must be good in bed too!**

The atmosphere is not one of freedom, but of growing demands on men and women. They need to be ever alert and available. Women are expected to have multiple orgasms, especially with vaginal penetration. Those who don't fake them. Men who are unable to get in the mood turn to medications, even when they are young. It is impossible to consider ourselves, in such a context, sexually freer than our parents (women nowadays being much less so than their mothers were).

I think the opposite: a sexually free man is one who is OK with himself even if he doesn't get an erection in a situation in which it was expected. I don't know many. They are free because they can fail to get an erection without feeling awkward, since sex is a context in which there shouldn't be any tension, duties, demands or obligations. The same thing is true for women, who will be free if they are able to explain that their orgasms are what they are and if the intensity of what they feel doesn't need to be measured by the number of decibels they produce. A free man is one who can say "yes" or "no" to a sexual opportunity. A free man is

Flávio Gikovate

one who decides to be faithful to his romantic partner and acts according to his convictions. Sexually free human beings are those who are not worried about their performance, don't compare themselves with outside standards or feel obliged to agree with points of view different to their own.

In order to think about freedom, we must strive to keep an active, rational mind that interferes and decides more than our biology, rather than blindly observing the norms and beliefs of the culture we live in – which we do for fear of rejection or because we don't have the courage to make our own mistakes, instead preferring to dilute ourselves in the mistakes of the majority. A free individual needs to have solid points of view, which can and must be mutable, able to adapt to new experiences and more precise conclusions, which, over the years, we can arrive at through the resources that porous brains use to learn.

A free individual doesn't follow standards that they don't approve of or which are in disagreement with the ideas they hold dear at the time. I repeat what I wrote in the early 1980s: being free isn't being this way or that; it is an inner joy that comes from being coherent, able to act in keeping with what we think.

FROM THE SAME AUTHOR

A LOVE STORY... WITH A HAPPY ENDING

Technological advances and changes in society have led to the growth of individuality and the impoverishment of conventional love – which nonetheless prevails in the collective imagination as an ideal. This slow transformation, according to Flávio Gikovate, is excellent news. He believes that adults today have two options, both of which are much better than the possessive conventional relationships of old: to live alone, establishing more superficial emotional and physical connections; or to develop relationships based on what he calls +love, which respects individuality and can create ties capable of lasting a lifetime. In this work, Gikovate explains how to take the second path – definitely more difficult, but far more rewarding.

FROM THE SAME AUTHOR

EVIL, GOOD AND BEYOND
The selfish, the generous and the fair

In Evil, Good and Beyond, Flávio Gikovate states that the union between man and woman is a bond between opposites — that is, a selfish person is bewitched by a generous person and the other way around. Yet this kind of relationship causes both partners problems, for they will ultimately go through situations of sorrow and disappointment. According to the author, investing in one's own freedom and individuality is the solution. This could give rise to couples made up of two fair people, more prepared to experience love.